IR

THE
MAMAS

THE
MAMAS

What I Learned About Kids, Class,
and Race from Moms Not Like Me

HELENA ANDREWS-DYER

CROWN
NEW YORK

Published in the United States by Crown, an imprint of Random House, a division of Penguin Random House LLC, New York.

CROWN and the Crown colophon are registered trademarks of Penguin Random House LLC.

Grateful acknowledgment is made to LeConté Dill for permission to reprint "The Fourth of You Lie" by LeConté Dill. Originally appeared on Zócalo Public Square (zocalopublicsquare.org) on May 19, 2021, and received honorable mention in the 10th annual Zócalo Poetry Prize. Reprinted by permission of LeConté Dill.

Hardback ISBN 978-0-593-24031-1
Ebook ISBN 978-0-593-24032-8

Printed in Canada on acid-free paper

crownpublishing.com
randomhousebooks.com

1 2 3 4 5 6 7 8 9

First Edition

Book design by Diane Hobbing

For Sally, Leta, Frenchie, Frances, me, Sally, and Robyn

CONTENTS

AUTHOR'S NOTE

Most of the names and identifying details in this book have been changed in order to protect the precious privacy of moms who don't need another damn thing to worry about.

INTRODUCTION

White girls made me do it. All right, *made* could be a pinch too much. Sounds a bit . . . you know. So, no. *Convinced? Cajoled? Conjured?* Because surely only a crazy person under the influence of blond spell work would respond to a WhatsApp invite to "meet up" before 9 A.M. and below 40 degrees thusly: "We'll be there!!!"

Blame it on the exclamation points. Their thirsty asses are the reason my fifteen-month-old daughter and I ended up bouncing for warmth around a socially distant circle of mostly white moms and their babies in the park formerly known as an open-air drug mart near the erstwhile frat house we call home. Robyn—that's my kid—is here for none of this. The child is screaming her head off in an obvious attempt to alert CPS, while I try to make small talk about the pre-K lottery with the think-tank director who essentially leads this gang of moms I got jumped into a few years ago after the birth of my older daughter earned me the right to membership. It's in this moment, as my baby's cheeks ice over with tears and I go on and on about ELA scores, that I realize we're like "a thing," me and these moms, and also that me and Robyn should probably leave before her fingers fall off. Wait, did I mention that I'm Black? Like, Black all the way through (whatever that means). And that the Blacks don't *do* this? The cold, I mean. Oh, and that stereotypes are still a thing?

Because if our collective common sense wasn't innate, then I wouldn't feel so 'shamed for depositing a popsicle disguised as a baby into the PPE-swathed arms of Miss Kim thirty minutes later. Miss Kim is the masked fairy charged with keeping my kid alive and who, I'm pretty sure, doesn't know my first name. Today Miss Kim is wearing a unicorn onesie with her Senegalese twists done up in the front like a horn, and when I hand her Robyn, I play off my baby's shrieking as monokerophobia. I'm two blocks away and *this close* to getting away with it when my back pocket starts barking.

"Hi, Mom!" *Shit.* "Mom? This is Miss Kim! Robyn's teacher?" We've spoken almost every day for a year and yet Miss Kim never fails to introduce herself anew over the phone, as if I could forget her in the tetherball-string length of time we spend apart.

"Yep," I reply, trying to sound super casual while hoping against hope that Robyn has an unexplained butt rash and not, like, hypothermia. "Everything okay?" See what I'm doing here? I *know.* I know my child is cold down to her bones. I know she is pissed about that fact. But I don't want Miss Kim, a middle-aged Black woman who embraces "Spirit Week" with the fervor of someone in possession of multiple adult-sized onesies, to know that I know. Because I don't want Miss Kim to know that I did it for the Mamas, a group of mothers I met on Facebook filled with the type of girls I used to make fun of in college and who, decades later, have clearly led me to forsake my Black-ass common sense.

"*Weeelll.*" Miss Kim is hesitant, afraid to wag her finger at me although I deserve it, because the three hundred dollars we shell out a week keeps her flush in furry one-pieces and whatnot. "Her little arms and legs are like ice! She just won't stop crying! Poor thing! Was she outside for a really long time this morning?" I know Miss Kim wants to suck her teeth.

This is the part where I—a fully grown woman who does not own onesies in her size and whose older daughter, Sally, believes chill pills are daily vitamins—consider lying. I can't tell Miss Kim that I was quite literally chilling with the white girls. She'd have my badge! Because it *is* cold today. So frigid, in fact, that when I told my husband, Rob, that I was strongly considering heading to the park to hook up with the stroller cartel for a pandemic-friendly "mom thing" and then walking the extra twelve blistering blocks to the Baptist church that houses our daycare, his response was an incredulous, "For what?" The better question would be for whom—the Mamas, Robyn, me? I'm still trying to figure out the new math involved.

Is the woman who has her baby out in the cold for no other reason than to cling to the fast-escaping steam of human connection the sum of all these parts—parenthood, race, class, status—or have they subtracted her? The real problem to tackle was a puzzle: How did a Black mom fit into the nearly all-white definition of motherhood that dominated the streets of her rapidly gentrifying D.C. neighborhood? Were these women I'd risk frostbite for my friends? Parenting colonizers? My competitors? Consider this book as the word problem to end all word problems. In the end, an answer should be forthcoming—or at the very least I'll show my work.

But first, there's this icy toddler to contend with.

Miss Kim, still trying to solve the mystery of the frozen baby, has had a stroke of genius. "Blankets!" she shouts. "We'll try to warm her up with blankets."

This woman is trolling me. I'm sure of it now. Because Black moms should know better. *We* see the temperature drop to "she needs a coat coat," and then it's a mad dash from inside to inside. Outside is a nonstarter, something to be avoided at all costs when the air suddenly goes visible. Let's say it has something to do with our equatorial origins or perhaps just the good sense God gave us. Either way, I've failed on both fronts, and Miss Kim, the same woman who must remind me to bring wipes for Robyn's asshole at least three times before it sticks, won't let this shit go.

"Matter of fact," she underlines, "I'm going to put some in the dryer right now. That should do it." She pauses, waiting for me to fill up the rest of this conversation bubble with self-flagellation.

Here's what I say: "Ugh, my poor little Robyn Bobbin. I'm sure she'll be all right. Thanks for calling. Have a great day." And here's what I want to say: *The child is fine! The Swedish leave their children outside in subzero temperatures while they get their hair done. It was in* Time *magazine. Google it! I'm a good mother!* What's even worse is the fact that my hypothermia hypocrisy is very hard-won.

See, in the Before Times (pre-children, pre–having cares in the world, pre-Covid), whenever a happy tribe of unapologetically white Maclaren moms crossed my path—bogarting the sidewalks, infiltrating cafés, touching things with their breeder hands—I'd do the sign of the cross, roll my eyes, and seal it with a heavy sigh. There but for the grace of God go I. I saw none of myself in them. White parents doing pirouettes with their hatless children on snowy sidewalks? I'd press my lips together, shake my head, and turn to Rob: "Ooowee, white people just love the cold, don't they?" "Ummhmm." Brandishing my imaginary fists at these insane parents, I'd TED-talk them in my head: "Get that baby in the house! It's freezing out! What is wrong with you?"

How'd it happen? How did I go from Judge Snooty Fox to what my husband called "full-on suburban white lady"? First off, he was joking. Obviously! Despite spending hours in the mirror stroking my fraying bath towel "hair" as a six-year-old, trust I ain't ever wanted to be anything but Black with a capital B, and I'd rather eat mayonnaise sandwiches every day for a year than move to the suburbs. See what I did there—the code-switching? That invisible see-saw is what parenthood is like for mamas like me who *technically* have more in common with the good white folks living in the million-dollar flip next door than the skinfolk barbecuing on their stoops down the block. Because there is no denying that being a middle-class Black mother to Black children in a neighborhood wobbling drunkenly on the gentrifying cliff of a thinned-out Chocolate City is a . . . different experience. An experience *other* parents are having around the country. An experience we hadn't really prepared for. An experience untold.

That's what this book aims to do. To "tell it," as Grandmommy would say. The story of what it's like being "the only one" in a Polly Pocket world of postracial parenting that primarily concerns itself with baby music class and not class divides. How hiding out there was both a welcome breather and a constant reminder. Because of course the world writ large came rushing in with a vengeance. A global pandemic both downsized our lives and expanded our world view. And just as we were wrapping our minds around what that meant, George Floyd happened. A man was murdered. A father who called out for his mama. And being a Black mother hit different. We were different. These women and I. Women who were raising the children my two baby girls would grow up around, play with, fight with—and one day hopefully survive. Sure, we were alike. They obsess over silly shit; they think their husbands are lazy; they work too much, feel guilty about it, and then feel guilty about the guilt, because feminism. But we're not the same. Not at all. Was admitting that fact unnecessarily divisive or desperately necessary?

For as long as I've been a mother, I've been on the hunt for "mom friends," collecting ladies with babies like grown-up baseball cards. When some dude (okay, fine, my husband) put a baby in me, my operating system (the one with the unwritten code about never being one of *those* moms) completely rebooted. Instantly the idea of a mom gang seemed like a smart survival tactic—like how they do in prison. And if there was one thing our neighborhood did not lack (aside from expensive-ass houses) it was ladies with babies. Filling up the long days of my privileged maternity leave by evil-eyeing the other inmates in the yard didn't seem like the best use of my sentence. Remember: do the time, don't let the time do you. We were all in this together, right? I jumped in.

That got me to the Really Big Question: Did motherhood truly connect us? And by *us* I'm not just talking about Black moms and white moms—although the dividing line there is sharp—but also Black moms of the Jack and Jill set and Black moms who set trip, moms across class divides, mothers from different sides of the aisle, you get the picture. Can we ever truly be friends, like really real friends? Not just mom friends or park friends or "Hey, sometimes I see you at the bodega struggling with your Boppy wrap too" friends? Or would there always be a chasm between us, whether it be cultural or cultivated, real or imagined? Would our tribes always win out? Would we be forced to choose? Did we need to in order to survive?

This book is me trying to answer questions I hadn't thought deeply about before double-Dutching in my midthirties to the nursery rhyme: "First comes love, then comes marriage, then comes the baby in the baby carriage!" Oh, and on the downbeat come gentrification, a global pandemic, racial justice, and my mom moving in. (Actually, no. This is a safe space. Guys, I never learned how to double-Dutch.) This book is for all the mamas trying to make sense of all that racket without getting tangled up in those ropes, falling flat on their faces. Field guide it is not. It is not a book explaining Black motherhood to white mothers. Or skewering Karenting. Or clapping for parents with #BLM signs in their front yards but zero Black friends to invite through their front doors. It's a story. My story. At its heart this book is about how the people surrounding us reflect the many versions of ourselves—whether they look like us or not, whether we want them to or not. It's about a tightrope walk, a mental load, a struggle unseen. It's the silent backstory we pack with us on trips to the park, the playground, the

PTA Zooms. It's for anyone who's been "the only one" and for those who claim not to notice.

The mamas. Who gets to decide membership? Who holds the annual meetings? The mamas. They're the amalgam of women I've clung to—the white moms of my changing neighborhood, the Black mom friends who sit together in the café, my own insane mother, and the one I look at in the mirror. All that is to say, I'm telling the story of finding my own identity as a woman with children through the women I leaned on, laughed with, and learned from. They've taught me that the lady I previously ignored on the street could be the same one I text my secret anxieties to, that all the measuring up we do just reveals more of our own shortcomings, and that kids scare us all shitless and make us brave. They've also taught me that mothering isn't a monolith and everyone isn't out to get us. And to never let your Black Mama guard down—ever. That true friends of any color have to earn your trust and prove themselves. Oh, and white people love the cold, don't they?

THE
MAMAS

CHAPTER 1

Group

It sounds so self-helpy, right? Mom group. So desperate. So fluorescent overhead lighting. So awkward folding-chair circles in Baptist church basements, with Styrofoam-flavored coffee. Women taking polite turns speaking their "truths" about cracked nipples, nutty grandmas, shitty babies, and FUPAs. I mean, in the end that's pretty much it. A bunch of strangers banding together to struggle through their shared obsession. "Group" as a verb. How super lame. How very uncool or urban or whatever random adjective got snipped from an old copy of *O: The Oprah Magazine* and glued to my mom vision board. There are so many stories we tell ourselves about who we are, who we're supposed to be, and who we should be with. To me "mom groups" always sounded like something for white women, period. But why? Are Black women not moms? Do we not love a good group?

To get to the bottom of those questions I asked my Black friends who are moms and who also happen to live all over the country to weigh in via a completely unscientific Google survey, because I was tired of texting. The responses I got from these women who unfortunately don't live down the street, and therefore can't be in my day-to-day mom clique, were equal parts hilarious and heartbreaking. One mom called her local group a "nice sanity check" and repeated the African proverb, "It takes a village." She had intentionally joined a group specifically designed "for Black mommas." Another mom, who knitted together an informal Black mom group, still said the very term was like nails on a chalkboard— "sounds like a bunch of white women doing stuff to make the world in the shape they want it for their specific kid." When asked who exactly "mom groups" were for, one mother answered, "Stay-at-home/gently employed white women who make Goldfish crackers from scratch and decorate their front porches for every season." This same mom admitted that "it would be nice to have women to get advice from and vent with" but her "wack" schedule wouldn't allow it, plus she didn't feel like being "judged by type A women." That was the general perception of the women who populate the twenty-first-century baby bee. When I mentioned maybe possibly joining my friendly neighborhood mom group, my day ones scoffed—like literally scoffed—at the idea. "For what?" But for real, wasn't I too, ummm, Black for this? Is that a thing? Didn't I know my own kind of people with babies? What would eleven-year-old Helena, who vowed never to let the sixth grade Stepford-wives-in-training make her feel small again, say about all this? Would she high-five me or slap some sense into me?

It began innocently enough.

After I got pregnant with my first daughter, Sally, one of my colleagues at *The Washington Post*, told me about this Facebook group I *had* to join: Bloomingdale Mamas. It was for all the ladies "in our hood," a zip code that was basically gentrification ground zero. We had been living in a cute condo in Bloomingdale for three years, and three-quarters of my take-home pay. Then two lines on a pregnancy test meant more space, and Rob and I managed to find a former party house to rent that had room for a baby. There were deep black gouges in the dining room floor, caused by either a pissed-off dragon or DJ equipment. No two doors were the same in size, functionality, or style. One closet smelled murder-y. And all the windows on the first floor were more decorative than operable.

But it had a "finished basement" for my mom, who planned on moving in to help us save money on daycare for a few months. (Who were we kidding? We were never going to be able to afford daycare.) The new house was on a quiet street curved like a rainbow and lined with single family homes. The block was dotted with elm and red maple trees—I know this because I looked them up. Grown-ups know the names of trees. One giant American elm shot up some sixty feet right in front of our house like a gnarly hand pulling down the sky. Tree-lined. That's a thing. We could carefully step out onto the rotting wood of our Wardman-style porch and hear birdsong instead of the homeless-man a cappella group in residence at the last condo we rented. It felt suburban. It felt like a step up, even with all the cracks. It felt like the kind of place parents would live.

So, the Bloomingdale Mamas, the online chrysalis from which I would emerge transformed. Because if it was all about the mothers of the neighborhood—the perfect backdrop to the family photos of the future—then I was all in. I had to be. Wasn't this my identity now? Helena, soon-to-be mother. Helena, in charge of vacuuming a three-story house and looking out onto our malaria swamp of a backyard and envisioning children therein. Helena, the grown. I joined the Mamas a full five months before my firstborn arrived.

After sending the group's moderator a message with an embarrassing exclamation-point-to-sentence ratio, this was my first post: "Lost Keys: I'm blaming my preggo brain on losing our old house keys somewhere along First Street between Channing and Florida

NW. If anyone happens upon them (they've got about four actual keys, one black electronic key and a *Washington Post* key ring) please ping me. Thanks!" I was announcing myself. Pregnant. Check. Lives in a house not an apartment. Check. Has a big important job. Check. Is very fun and self-deprecating. Check. What was happening to me? Was I so desperate for validation from randos? Yes, yes I was. Thankfully, that post got zero likes, hearts, sad faces, or comments, which further proves the theory that obsessively checking Facebook does not make the comments come faster. I found my keys in the front yard later that day, but I kept it pushing. The Facebook group was still a nut that needed cracking into.

Plus, there were the offshoots to consider. There was a neighborhood parent email listserv that required your full government name and address to join lest you be some outside-the-zip interloper sneakily devouring posts about the local soccer league and summer nanny shares. There was even another spin-off Facebook group aimed at "new moms" who wanted to "meet up" once the weather got nice, and an additional email list for the same. Workouts in the park for the shrinking of postbaby bodies. Library story time you had to get tickets for in advance. There was also a new language to learn—FS (for sale), FFPPU (free for porch pick up), and ISO (in search of)—because the baby-crap black market is booming among folks who could definitely afford to click "buy now." Plus, loads of advice (all fervently solicited) to comb through about sleep training, pumping, and "school lottery-ing." There were hundreds of members, more moms than I knew existed in our two-by-thirteen-block wedge of Washington, and hardly any of them Black, which was eerie considering we lived in walking distance of Howard University. The Facebook group was like an alternative dimension where the realities of the world outside rarely made an appearance, except in the annual Fourth of July posts entitled "Fireworks or Gunshots?"

Once Sally landed on solid ground, lurking online became my favorite maternity-leave pastime aside from, you know, taking care of her. I'd logged on from the maternity ward right after my daughter was born, despite my best efforts to stay off the internet for six weeks in accordance with my "confinement"—a Chinese postpartum practice I learned about on the internet. But there I was in my hospital bed, thumbing through post after post as if they were puzzle pieces that, collected together, might make this whole motherhood thing make sense. And there I was at home on our hand-me-down couch with a tiny Sally nestled in the crook of one arm while I stared at the palm-sized idiot box cradled in my other hand. This wasn't neglect, okay? This was me learning—as vital as the baby books stacked in a totem pole by my side of the bed.

But as much as I craved my daily (fine, hourly) peeks into the lives of women who looked nothing like me but were living near parallel lives to mine (married, working, crashing), I also resented their freedom. I don't know what else to call it. Here was a forum for all things big and small—clothing swaps, home-renovation advice, wake times—that was clearly so necessary, a ray of light for creepo postpartum Gollums like myself. But it was also so blindingly white, and so unaware or unconcerned or even to blame for that fact. What was I doing caring so much about these thumbnails? Was I buying into the lily-white version of motherhood or disrupting the feed with my presence? Oh, the internal conflict! Like these women, I had briefly imagined myself better than I was and considered cloth diapers. Emily Oster, the economist turned "you can drink wine while pregnant" evangelist, was also my spiritual guide. I was dutifully steaming and blending organic vegetables that painted pretty pictures on our dining room wall at dinnertime. Being Black didn't inoculate me from being a maniac. There wasn't some latent mammy gene that made me an expert on child-rearing and therefore not prone to poking my kid ten times in as many minutes to make sure she was still breathing. I needed this space as much as they did. Who didn't?

The inescapable fact that the vast majority of all these "mamas" were white really pissed me off. It felt like an exclusive club where motherhood and whiteness were one and the same. It gnawed at me. The babymoon was over. Enter my hate-scrolling phase. I spent precious downtime shitting on said group and all the unknowable women therein. It was like a nervous tic or something.

"They're going to 'stroller strides' on Wednesday. Stroller strides?!" I'd call from the couch as Sally napped in her swing nearby. "Bitch, y'all walking real fast around the block! Why does everything suddenly have a new alliterative name?"

"Just say you want to go. It's fine." That's Rob, my husband, for whom the politics of mom-grouping is not, and never will be, a thing.

"I don't," I shot back.

Silence.

"I don't! I swear."

"So unsubscribe then, crazy." Why, oh why, do men offer up solutions nobody asked for to problems no one has?

"No. No. I have to know what's going on. I *need* to be informed," I maintained. "Plus, I can't go anyway. We didn't get the jogging stroller. It was too pricey, remember?"

"White people are cheap!" I shouted apropos of nothing.

"In what way?" Rob asked.

"All they do is give stuff away or ask each other for stuff 'before I buy new,'" I exclaimed while scrolling through a gaggle of posts proving my point. "They don't wanna spend any money. This is how they stay rich."

"Ummhmm."

"I'm serious."

"Okay."

"Someone is giving away her nursing bras. Bras!"

"What size?"

"It doesn't matter, fool. That's nasty."

"Right."

"Now they're up in arms about that shooting on W," I point out, even though I was similarly indignant the night before. "Like, hello, we live in D.C."

"You know that's not normal, right?" said Rob.

"What's not normal?"

"Shootings. Like, that isn't something folks should want to get used to. Ever."

"We are!"

"No, no we are not."

We went around and around like this for weeks. Me reading aloud all the alleged faults I found with the Mamas and dragging my slightly amused husband along for the ride. He'd only taken two weeks off when Sally was born, so he owed me. Six weeks into maternity leave, I still hadn't met the mothers I'd been stalking for months. I could point to the Big Ole Race Thing, but it's not like I didn't have white friends. Who doesn't? I could say it was the class divide, but hadn't I crossed that bridge busing into private school for over a decade, followed by the Ivy League, the master's, the legacy media job? I could claim the utter uncoolness of it all, but seriously, grow up. Despite all my arguments to the contrary, I knew these women would help usher me through the isolation of the newborn stage, the next five months of leave, the transition back to work, and then the endless debate about "the next one."

At thirty-seven, I thought I was done making new friends. Full stop. There were already too many boxes cluttering up my friend closet—the day ones, the homies from high school, the friends from college, the work wives and husbands, the neighbor friends, the liquor store friends, and now the mom friends. Marie Kondo would not approve. I kept trying to talk myself out of the whole thing. Weren't mom friends the worst of the bunch? Like you, they've expelled a screaming life-form from their bloated bodies and lived to tell the gunky tale. Can you imagine a grosser icebreaker?

Really, there is no relationship as flammable as the female friendship—at least that's what the man would have us believe, to keep us apart like Mister did Celie and Nettie. *Catty, bitchy, judgy.* Those are the adjectives we get. All versions of the same alleged problem—women don't mix well. Add in postpartum hormones and the cocktail has the potential to poison. But mom friends were supposed to be different. They were supposed to make the whole experience, this life change, more bearable, right? So shouldn't I feel less excluded, afraid, and stupid when considering them? I swear, after an obligatory awkward phase, I had all the friends in high school. All of them. But something about making new female friends in adulthood turned me into that bumbling dork who breastfeeds alone in a restaurant while a cemented squad of ladies with babies laughs hysterically a few tables away. It was like a private club. I should've been let in; my membership card was strapped to my chest. But I couldn't walk up to the gate.

To cope, I'd convinced myself that as the loud and proud only child of a loud and proud lesbian single mother I didn't need no stinking regressive women's-only club that reinforced the patriarchal view that mothers do all the work. Wasn't I raising a feminist!

I'd show her by werewolfing myself. Plus, I was used to being my own best friend. Lots of latchkey-kid alone time will do that to you. Watching *The Handmaid's Tale* with the baby was revolutionary. Until it wasn't. After a few weeks' protesting at home, I gave up the fight, longing as I was for some sustained daytime adult interaction that wasn't lunch with a childless friend who, let's face it, was completely useless, or a friend with giant older kids who might as well have been baby-eating trolls. The Facebook group was *riiight* there. The women lived within walking distance. All I had to do was actually go to one of the outings the New Moms thread kept going on about. They were meeting in the park, at the beer garden, the coffee shop, the movie theater. I just had to show up and declare myself one of them. Why was that so hard?

Well, there were a lot of reasons. My insecurities—both real and imagined—for one thousand. Motherhood so often gets sugarcoated through a white lens. They've got June Cleaver, Donna Stone, Murphy Brown, hell, even Daenerys Targaryen. We've got Clair Huxtable. Oh, and Michelle Obama. Perfect and perfect, such a range. Switch over to the nightly news and the spectrum gets stretched to include welfare queens and baby mamas. I wasn't just afraid to go, my feet were reluctant participants—weighed down by stereotypes no one admits out loud but that play on a mental loop all the same. And as the only Black girl in the group, I had to be twice as good at something we all suck at.

One day, not too long after we brought my daughter home, while my mom and I watched Rob outsmart yet another useless baby contraption, Frances casually let slip that she'd been on welfare for a year after I was born. After seeing my reaction, which in my defense I am not proud of, she immediately started backpedaling. "I mean, I looked for a job. I did! But I'd left you at one babysitter's with like five diapers, right? And when I came back at the end of the day, all five were still in the bag," she remembered with a quiet blue chuckle as my husband "Jesus" and "Christ"ed his way through instructions. My mother explained that she figured staying home was the smarter move. "You never told me that," I said, trying not to let my voice crack. Frances shrugged her shoulders, letting the memory roll off her back, and then grabbed a box cutter to slice open the next package from Amazon.

We overcompensate. It's the reason why every name we considered for Sally had to pass "the résumé test." It's why Beyoncé, a woman who folks accused of faking a pregnancy, went full on Father/Mother Earth Goddess while carrying twins and why Serena Williams, who folks accused of faking being a woman, posed for the cover of *Vanity Fair* belly butt-naked like biiiiih. Black motherhood has been exploited, erased, vilified, and denied, so it's no wonder that when we choose it, we go fucking ham.

Which brings me to my next point. Wanna hear about the time I *almost* murdered my firstborn child? I was trying to *mother*. Like, a verb.

After stalking them online for weeks, I finally decided to shut up and show up to one of the group's "fun activities"—a "crybaby matinée" of the garbage film *Baywatch*. There was just one thing standing between me and success—the K'tan. K'huh? Never heard of it? Like most newborn gadgets, the K'tan—or the Boba, or the MOBY, or all the other vaguely ethnic-sounding baby wraps out there—is a deceptively simple method of mental torture. Remember those "convertible" dresses that were basically just yards and yards of fabric that promised dozens of different styles so long as you had a PhD in human origami? Yeah, the K'tan is sort of like that—an instant idiot quiz marketed to unsuspecting millennial women who normally crave instant gratification. The K'tan consists of two large loops of fabric held together by a smaller loop that you wear around your torso like a breastplate and that is just as fearsome. After countless YouTube videos and a few test runs involving an empty water jug as a Sally stand-in, I got my baby in that sucker and triumphantly set out for the movie theater about a mile and a half away. My baby, strapped to my chest and stomach, was safe and secure, and I was a fucking superhero. Our friendly corner-store loiterers spotted me catwalking down North Capitol Street and pointed to my middle. "Eh, you got a baby in there, sis?" I responded with a highfalutin head nod. Yes, yes, I do got a baby in here! Making my way through the D.C. streets, I was a mom on fire.

Did I mention it was the middle of June? Nearly 90 degrees? I conveniently ignored the sweat snaking from my brow to my neck and down the valley of my tits, a salty River Nile. Sally, her tiny body pressed to my human space heater, was looking a little wet herself, but that could just be nerves, right? We were out! Finally. Don't ruin this, kid. About halfway there it was clear that humidity, infant, and fabric did not go well together. Why would I carry a squirming eleven-pound animal straitjacketed against my engorged boobs? Because I wanted to prove to a bunch of white girls I'd never met that I could. I could mother like all the other women I was surrounded by, with the latest overpriced gadgets and ding-dongs meant to make you feel accomplished. So, no, I did not do the smart thing and turn back to seek the refuge of our window unit. We kept it pushing, power walking through the panic as I blew my hot breath on Sally in the hope that it'd cool her down. This was dumb. I knew it. But I kept going.

Once we finally got to the theater, baby girl was sopping wet. Not soaking. Sopping. It was bad. Real bad. Like "Why would someone try to waterboard a baby?" bad. And "Is the side of her face supposed to be that red?" bad. The six o'clock news kept replaying in my head as I rushed to the bathroom to get her out of that $59.99 death wrap. She slid off my chest like a drunken slug as I whirled her around the ladies' room thinking the stale air would help. It didn't. Long story short, the kid got overheated. She puked.

I cried. And the two of us sat sobbing in a stinking bathroom stall at the movie theater.

After the credits rolled (yes, we stayed to watch that dumb-ass movie), I fled in shame to the nearest coffee shop, the very place all the moms went afterward, bulldozing in with their gigantic jogging strollers like a biker gang. They boobed their babies while sipping lattes, performing a choreographed dance number I like to call "We're All Really Good Mom Friends." It looked complicated and beautiful, and I'd never—including that time in eighth grade when I spent a month's worth of lunch periods perfecting the Tootsee Roll—wanted so badly to learn a new step. Here I was, more than two decades later, huddled somewhere in the way way back to feed my dehydrated child free of judgment. One mom—later I learned her name was Meghan—glanced in our direction expectantly, and before our eyes could awkwardly lock, I quickly turned to gaze lovingly into Sally's. The kid was asleep. I was a fraud.

We waited there until long after their table had cleared out—until the temperature had safely dipped below "Keep old people and babies inside"—and then the two of us hobbled home together, deflated.

"Just try again next week," suggested Rob in his dumb man way.

"They'll recognize me! You think there are any other Black chicks in this thing?"

"So what? Just tell them you have social anxiety. They'll get that," he said before shrugging and adding, "White girls," as if that explained it. Perhaps it did.

I grew up the only Black girl in our small town of two thousand—and by *only,* I mean only. Look up the census data of the city of Avalon on Santa Catalina Island from 1986 to 1991, and you'll find two checked boxes for Black—me and Frances, my mom. So I spent an inordinate amount of time in elementary school being jealous of sun-freckled little girls with blond highlights. Maybe *jealous* isn't the word. More like *obsessed*. Or *fascinated? Enthralled? Enraged?* All those things. I don't know. Either way, I clocked in and out of an existence run by girls who didn't look like me, observing how they worked. What they wore—shell necklaces, checkered Vans, or Uggs, even in the 70-degree weather. What they said—*like* and *bitch* and *my gah*. And how they moved about the world in general—not so much as if they owned it but as if it owed them. There was this one girl, Wendy, a sharp-tongued elf of a sixth grader whose moods came to determine how my days would go. Aha! Meghan—the girl from the movies in more metaphors than one— reminded me of a grown-up Wendy. Innocent-looking yet quietly powerful and universally cheered.

White girls. They were my muses and my tormentors before I knew any better, dominating my frame of reference for . . . everything. Remember, we lived on an island. There was no escape. Even with a lesbian, hippie, super-Black mom who let me read *The Color Purple* at ten and once snatched the "pretend hair" towel off my head when she caught me preening in the bathroom mirror. "What grows out of your own dang head is perfectly fine!" After I finished elementary school we moved from Santa Catalina to South Central, and the culture shock was like a defibrillator's zap reviving a racial identity that had flatlined. Thank God for the Black girls in seventh and eighth grade who teased and dragged my sense of self into existence. By puberty I'd learned that other women could either bulldoze or rebuild, and safe havens weren't hard to come by as long as you knew where to look. The mirror was a good start. Imagine then the cold shock that came when nearly thirty years later, after growing up and allegedly growing past the white girl gaze, I once again found myself submerged in it.

But I wasn't a kid anymore. I was a grown-ass woman with direct deposit, a whole husband, and a baby I'd planned. Dipping my feet into the mommy pool of Bloomingdale didn't mean I'd drown, right? Right? I figured holding my nose and diving in was better than doggy-paddling alone in the deep end. Okay, enough with the water metaphors. In the end, I knew I had more in common with these women than I wanted to admit and that admitting it didn't make me less Black, down, militant, or whatever. I'd googled "Gwyneth Paltrow's pregnancy" and pinned a million images of "gender neutral" nurseries too. And Black card not revoked, because there isn't a government agency for that. I was assuming that their pins weren't so much aspirational as they were shopping lists. While I, on the other hand, was trying to outrun a lifetime (make that generations) of poor-kid impostor syndrome. They'd all grown up in the kinds of homes that produced Gerber babies and *Family Ties* plot lines. Hadn't they?

All this mental hemming and hawing was mine alone. No one, besides maybe Rob, knew the angst bubbling up in my guts and polluting my breast milk (if internet chat rooms were to be believed). All these big questions were swimming around in there when I finally got out of my own way long enough to make it safely to our first official mom meetup (I took a mulligan on that *Baywatch* debacle). According to the Facebook group, there was a regular mom hang at Crispus Attucks Park, a reclaimed acre of gentrified grass hiding between four city alleys. It was named after a formerly enslaved man who was the first to be killed in the Boston Massacre of 1770, which subsequently kick-started the American Revolution. So, like, no weird racial stuff going on there. Sally and I arrived in perfect condition for adult circle time under a tree. That's how most mom group meetings shape up—an impromptu ring of swaddle cloths, coffee-shop chairs, or strollers. Circles are binding. They're strong. Impenetrable.

As I walked up with Sally strapped expertly, and dressed weather-appropriately, in her K'tan, I did the requisite scan of the crowd, immediately clocking that we were the "only ones"—a state of

being most Black folks are used to. This, of course, put me on alert
to dial it down, be nonthreatening, Black but not *too* Black, basically never too comfortable. I didn't know these women.

We introduced ourselves baby first. "Hi, this is Sally and I'm—"
Nobody cares, Helena! At this fragile rung of conditional friendship,
there is only one character trait that really matters—your tiny
human proxy. Their names, ages, genders (or non), poop color,
rolling-over ability, potential career choices, etc. The whole thing
reminded me of when I used to go to the dog park with my pug,
Miles, and the disparate group of weirdos known as dog owners
would stand around commenting on their pet's ability to do people
things. Now we actually had little humans, but weren't they still
just wild animals who couldn't talk? Here's what we talked about on
those bright Wednesday mornings:

- Doulas, like a basketball coach but for your cooch
- Why cry-it-out is absolutely not child abuse . . . when
  you're white
- Nanny shares, or how to find out how much other people
  make
- Music class, because you gotta have rhythm to co-opt the
  future
- Pre-K lotteries, in which gambling is not only acceptable—
  it's encouraged
- "Two under two" or "The condom broke, and we were
  just, like, whatever"

Much like the night I lost my virginity, the whole thing was a
memorable blur. What we talked about mattered less than how we
talked about it—with a familiarity and ease only real friends should
have. Boobs were out and loose. Tongues even more so. Vaginas were
discussed. Surgeries dissected. Extreme exhaustion went unmasked.

I even asked the woman next to me, who'd just gone into the gory details of her harrowing birth story with the women next to her, "Did you guys know each other? Before?" Because my God. The fact that *I'd* overheard that she'd almost died after two blood transfusions seemed like an invasion of privacy. "Oh no," she said. "We met here last week." Not ten minutes later I was deep into a conversation about how my mother, who was living with us for the year, was driving me completely nuts. "Oh my God, me too," replied the girl I had confided in, my ten-minute best friend. "My mother is a fucking maniac," she said. We smiled at each other while bouncing our babies to sleep. Just when I thought I wasn't one of them, they pulled me in.

You've heard of the boiling frog metaphor, right? The theory starts off like this: Put a live frog in 100-degree-Celsius water and it will immediately hop out, because duh. Why would a fly-eating fun-loving frog, who was otherwise minding her green-ass business, suddenly decide to end it all simply because the opportunity presented itself? Self-preservation and all that. But the metaphor doesn't end there. Say you really want this frog to take its final bath. Instead of chucking it into boiling water, try placing it gently into a tepid soak, then slowly but surely raise the temperature degree by degree from spa to slaughterhouse. The frog won't know what hit her. The change is imperceptible—right until it's not.

After that first meetup in the park I was officially cooked. I hadn't found my "people" per se, but I'd found something more than just a simple distraction, the treasure after all that creepy Facebook digging. People. Real live people. Within weeks, maternity leave was starting to feel as dreamy as that summer Sandy spent with Danny Zuko. Eventually I got the hang of things and became a full-fledged Mama, dutifully showing up to our tree in the park with my pristine eight-week-old child and making small talk for an hour with women who'd previously passed me on the street without a second glance. I began to open up, excavating my hopes and anxieties and frustrations and joys as a new mom in front of these women because they were available, if not exactly my type. Sure, our meetups were ridiculous and bougie, but I looked forward to them every week, waking Sally up if she was napping so that we'd make it on time. In that little hidden park, these women showed me this shadow world—one free of men, demanding bosses, and, for a time, racial anxiety—that I reveled in. And it wasn't just the free therapy—the necessity of which can't be understated. Park meetups soon turned into Mondays at the Ethiopian coffee shop, middle-of-the-week music class, and baby yoga sessions on Friday, which always led to lunch and a long, lingering stroller ride home with someone new to confide in. These bitches took up my whole week! And I didn't mind one bit.

There was Jenn, who liked to kick each meeting off with a question that not-so-subtly revealed everyone's "status" (socioeconomic or otherwise), like "So how are you handling kitchen remodel *and* the new baby?" Then there was the Other Jenn (the Mom Vet), who was on baby number two, wore Daisy Dukes with abandon, and repeatedly soothed my fear that an ant would crawl into Sally's ear if I laid her on the ground like everyone else did their kids. "And then what would happen?" she would ask. Leah was a professional hippie, in the best way, whose regular Instagrams of family mountain treks are the reason there's currently a hiking baby carrier collecting dust in our basement. Her commitment to the connection between bare feet, dirt, and energy reminded me of my mom's "healing white light philosophy," which often replaced Tylenol in our house growing up. Carly appeared to be a trust-fund kid who worked herself to the bone to hide that fact. She'd been hit with the Shit Got Real wand and experienced every nightmare newborn scenario there was—nipple confusion, colic, sleep regression, you name it. The poor girl was exhausted and clinging to our meetups like they were NoDoz pills. Tiffany was an infectious disease doctor from a Mountain Dew town in Appalachia who would later convince me that face masks were bad for verbal skills. I admired her pluck, if not her occasional Trumpian slip. And, my personal fave, Mira, had a voice like Janeane Garofalo, with the midnineties nihilism to match. I ran into her once at the playground and watched slightly horrified as her daughter happily munched on a nearby tree. Mira just shrugged her shoulders. "She must be hungry."

And, of course, there was my grown-up Wendy: Meghan, whose daughter's name I gave up trying to pronounce—and who I believe secretly hated me for that fact. In my defense, this was my one-woman protest against name discrimination. White folks could name their kids any collection of letters in the known alphabet and everyone else just dealt. But let a mom of any other color get "creative" with spelling and pronunciation and such, and suddenly your baby is unbankable. (For the record, Sally's name has deep family history *and* is résumé-approved.) Anyway, Meghan. She had a resting bitch face, like me, and a designer diaper bag, unlike me. She posted on Facebook about donating school supplies to kids who'd been separated from their families, and all I could think was "of course" before opening my PayPal. What's the opposite of a Woman Crush Wednesday? A Made-Up Competition Monday? In the story of my life, she was my literary foil but had no idea. In the beginning her omnipresence—bouncy and blue-eyed—would make me go all scrunch face whenever I spotted her dipping into the expensive Italian place next to the bodega next to the yoga studio with her Botero baby in tow. Never able to put my finger on why she bugged me, I just assumed we weren't the right charge. Some people just don't magnetize, you know. Destined to push rather than pull. Something about her bleeding heart/renovated row house just rubbed me the wrong way. I felt judged even though it was me doing the judging.

The Mamas. Like a monster that eventually makes you laugh. They weren't scary, and I happily made room for them because they were a respite from everything else—work, husband, my "real" friends. I knew something had changed when I started referencing these former strangers in polite conversation elsewhere. "Well, my friend Meghan." *Wait, what? Your friend?* Yeah, I think so.

CHAPTER 2

Drinking the Cognac

Entrance into the hallowed halls of Mamahood was, of course, predicated on one nonnegotiable: You had to have a baby. That was the first barrier of entry. A hurdle that for years I'd sidestepped for reasons both practical and ephemeral. For me the very concept of conception was fraught with anxiety, which was rooted in race and class in a way that I had never been forced to truly investigate. That is, until more than half a dozen of my so-called friends—traitors, I call 'em—got knocked up in the same number of months, and suddenly the spotlight was on my own skittish uterus.

"I'm calling DC Water and getting our shit shut *off*!" Rob announced from the sink, bitch-slapping the gooseneck faucet for emphasis. A metallic ping echoed through the kitchen/dining/living room of the condo we rented. We were just two years in then. Young and dumb and afraid, so very afraid. "There's something in the water!"

"I can't fucking believe this!" I screamed from the couch, scanning the email that had sent us into panic mode for the fifth time, lip-reading every syllable to make sure I'd understood. "Like what are *we* doing wrong?"

"You mean 'right,'" Rob corrected. "What are we doing 'right'!"

Now he was on his way to the couch with a tumbler filled half-way with amber liquid. I hated the brown stuff, but I loved Rob, a six-foot-four-inch Midwesterner who would take charge in a crisis like this.

"We're drinking nothing but yak from here on out," said Rob, handing me the glass of fancy French brandy like it was medicine. "No more water for you." I reached for it without taking my eyes off my laptop. I'd read the fucking email six times.

"It's like an epidemic," I said, before taking a swig and shaking my head at the sudden sting.

"Yak. From. Now. On."

This is how we used to react to other people's pregnancy news. By drinking Cognac, because clearly there was something in the water.

Frantic, bordering on hysterical. As if someone had just announced over the crackling school PA system that the vampire zombie wolves were making their way down the halls and all anyone had time for was one last gulp of preapocalyptic air.

At this point in the story the two of us were in our early thirties, and although the diaper-free world as we knew it had been quietly imploding for years—an overpriced bachelorette "weekend" here, the rare baby shower for that couple that got married *waaay* too young there—this latest bump announcement seemed precipitous. The terror alert had gone from green to red while we were in the janitor's closet making out. Two teenagers innocently groping in the dark one minute, then stumbling out into the bright lights of a bloody, undead stampede the next. Shouldn't we just duck back into the closet like nothing had happened?

It'd been two years since Rob and I met at a D.C. bar. He hates when I describe our meet-cute that way—"at a bar"—not because it's a cliché, but because it gets us only halfway there. Ever the annoyingly truthful middle American, Rob prefers that I say we were introduced "at brunch." It sounds much more civilized than "I met my eventual husband while drunkenly scream-singing the wrong lyrics to Color Me Badd's 'I Wanna Sex You Up.'" But that's also true.

It was the spring of 2010, and a glossy lady mag had just published an article about me and my first book, a collection of essays called *Bitch Is the New Black*. My friends and I—all grown up but just barely—got more amazing by the mimosa and were spending the afternoon waving a copy of the magazine around Vinoteca, the U Street bar that served as our personal "The Pit." A few stools down, a melanin-rich *m-a-n* in a Kansas City Royals cap looked up from his iPad just as my girlfriend Gizele shouted, "She's famous, by the way!" "Brotha" was the best way to describe him and absolutely no one under forty still said "brotha" then. What was this? *Waiting to Exhale? Boomerang? Love Jones?* Yes, times three. Because that's exactly what Rob was—a brotha. Tall for anywhere, not just D.C., skin like velvet, with a booming laugh and a goatee that looked sharpied on. Remember when we used to say "foine"? I remember wondering about him as he smiled at me, shaking his head at our weekend ritual of talking too loud and singing off-key. Brunch was a personality trait in those days.

I'd been dating someone who never understood why my Sundays were permanently blocked off. "You'd rather spend all day getting drunk with your friends," he spat at me during another fight I was only half listening to. He was a midlevel Hill staffer who "knew all the Obama people" and assured me that we could "win" together, whatever that meant. Then he referred to me once as "the missus" and I visibly cringed. This wasn't *him*. That was obvious. But I felt selfish throwing him back. I mean, how many chances was I going to get? A season later and seriously single, I began my search for "that big guy in the blue hat" who'd laughed at my drunken squad on Sundays past. His name was Rob, Jarrell the Bartender offered after my hounding. Then he added, "And you probably won't be able to handle him." It would be another six months before I proved him wrong.

It was the brunch before Valentine's Day. Rob showed up and sat by himself at the bar for hours, messing around on an iPad back when no one really had one. *What a fucking weirdo. Also, what was taking him so long to come over and sweep me off my feet!* The mimosas had hit rock bottom before he decided to make a move, pulling the finally empty stool next to me between his legs and ordering a round for the both of us without even looking my way. *What an ass. Also, when were we going to get married?* Don't ask me what we talked about. But I know it was easy. So easy that when my friends interrupted to say, "Oh, goodbye," I barely noticed brunch had ended.

Rob walked me the ten or so blocks to my upmarket condo building smooshed between a shady gas station and a liquor store. And that was that. He emailed me handwritten notes—like literally he wrote them on that damn iPad and then sent me PDFs. He bought me butter pecan ice cream. Dog-sat Miles when I was out of town and somehow taught him to walk up the scary-steep open staircase. "You have to carry him up every time," I'd warned. "Yeaaaaah, I am not doing that."

"Rob's here, don't be weird," I told a group of friends who'd come over to watch the Oscars back when we had the kind of free time to invite friends over for that sort of thing. "Remember homeboy we all met at Vino? Yeah, I took him home that night and he never fucking left." To their credit, when my crew walked in to find six feet four inches and 230 pounds of man posted up on my couch all comfortable-like in a cutoff T-shirt and that one pair of sweats he refuses to throw away, everyone just went with it. *Impressive,* their head nods seemed to say. He just was. Because the transition was so seamless, so natural, we hadn't realized we were living together until way after the fact.

But in the bathroom one morning it all became disgustingly clear.

"Babe, I need you," Rob called through the door.

"Absolutely not! I'm not gonna fall for a banana in the tailpipe!" I yelled back from the bedroom, already holding my breath, prepping to head to him in the bathroom.

"I'm serious," he said. "I can't do this alone."

Rob was standing in front of the mirror twisting his torso like an acrobat. "I can't get this bump."

"'Zit'! You mean 'zit.' And what am I supposed to do about it?"

As I stood there squeezing the skin on his back, I knew Rob and I were in it for the long haul. The thin wall separating us popped like that damn stubborn pimple, and at the very same time I couldn't help but shout, "Oh, this is a thing!" Rob laughed, agreeing as he handed me a square of toilet paper to clean up the gunk. Yep, definitely a thing.

The idea of marriage and babies and big life stuff was always in the background; we knew it was coming. But the tidal wave, nay tsunami, that greeted us at the shore was something else. Two years together felt like the appropriate time to start *thinking* about changing our legal statuses and my birth control prescription. But time was just a silly construct, right?

In fact, by the time we got "that email" we'd been living together longer than my latest pregnant friend—the source of our baby freak-out/yak binge—had actually known the father of her unborn child. While all the other brave fools were charging headfirst into the hoard of vampire zombie wolves, knowing full well it would be

their last stand, Rob and I were somewhere in the way way back
with our fingers shoved in our ears, singing, "La, la, la, laaaaa."

Us? Parents? Pass that brown.

Up until the fifth (fine, ninth) grade, I had it on good authority
that boys just peed in you and that's how you got pregnant, sort of
like watering a plant. I can't remember the exact moment I learned
the difference between urine and semen, but it didn't make the
process any more enticing.

About a month after one of my best friends, Adrienne, announced
she was pregnant, I got a text from a fellow non-knocked-up friend
with more good bad news: "Ash is preggers. Just so you know," and
then ten seconds later she sent a follow-up: "Oh, and Lindsay too."
There is no "I hope this doesn't become like a thing" emoji. If there
were it'd probably be a cartoon of a bloated belly surrounded by a
bold red circle with a diagonal line drawn across like how they do
for other dangerous habits like smoking. Also, that made three.
Shortly after that breaking baby news (BBN, let's call it) and also
via text, my good friend Jackie, who had been vehement about
never wanting kids ever, said she was pregnant. So much for stick-
to-it-iveness.

My friend from high school, Jessica, was unwittingly two weeks
pregnant when she and her husband stayed with me and Rob for
Barack Obama's 2013 inauguration festivities. We know this
because when they shared the good news a few months later, Rob
immediately started counting backward in order to make sure no
babies had been conceived "on or around our stuff." We were nothing if not vigilant.

At Adrienne's baby shower later that summer, between the oohs
and ahhs of opening presents, my sorority sister Evelyn pulled me
to the side. "It's still super early, but I didn't want you to be the last
to know." This was her second and now my sixth.

Rob and I were hanging on by a thread when that email came through. In it my girl Melissa kept using what I would quickly learn was not the royal "we" before finally announcing that she was five months pregnant. Five months.

The crazy thing—there were several, in fact—was that Melissa didn't bother to put the word *pregnant* in the subject line, as if it weren't the most outrageous news ever. She'd committed what every professor I had in J-school warned was a cardinal sin—burying the lede. It was perhaps the purest example of why the practice of not getting to the point is so infuriating in the first place. There I was innocently scrolling through an email chain about the weather, like literally we were complaining about how "hot as balls" it was during a record heat wave and trying to plan a trip to a public pool, when Mel dropped this bomb: "We were inside keeping cool. And by 'we,' let me clarify . . ."

The rest, obviously, is what sent me into hysterics—and what prompted our household ban on water.

The *other* crazy thing about my seventh friend in a row coming up pregnant—besides, well, just that—was the fact that I'd seen Melissa almost every single week since she'd conceived and had absolutely no clue anything out of the ordinary was happening with her insides. We had been fellow bridesmaids in a wedding, which is like saying we'd served in Operation Desert Storm together. Trying to bring peace to the Middle East and planning a drama-free bachelorette weekend in Atlantic City is essentially the same kind of thing. So maybe what drove me so nuts, more than the idea that she'd gone from normal to knocked-up in the course of an email, was that Melissa and I had been on the same side just one click ago. Now I was out there on my own. Left behind. Also, who the hell can wear Daisy Duke jorts when they're five months pregnant and just, like, blend in? It was annoying.

Betrayal is a strong word but an apt one. I kept doing that horrible thing you do when you break up with someone: replaying every single conversation you ever had in the hopes of uncovering some clue as to what went wrong. Like the time I asked a mimosa-less Melissa point-blank if she was pregnant and she said, "No," without blinking.

Thankfully, Rob was there to get me drunk, which might have been how all this started for some of my friends. I don't know if he was trying to drown out the pain or what, but it didn't work. Nothing, not even yak, could distract from the obvious, that for the rest of 2013 one of my friends would be giving birth every month. It was like the opposite of what my period had been for most of my grown-up life—a regularly scheduled reminder that all was going well with my general plan to avoid getting pregnant at all costs. But now I'd been forced to acknowledge my uterus. And after years of experiencing fear, loathing, or apathy toward it, I was feeling sorry for it.

If my uterus could talk about that particular era in our lives, I wonder what it would say. "Umm, hellooo, don't forget about me!" Or "Forget this!" while it packed its bags—off to some better body that appreciated it. Wanted it. Worried about it more. I don't know, maybe my uterus liked being left alone. Maybe it's agoraphobic, and all the fuss being made over it that year just gave it panic attacks, made it break out in hives.

We incorrectly assumed that, much like allergy season, the baby boom would go away on its own eventually, making room for the first house boom or the promotion boom. But it didn't. The hits just kept coming and all the yak in the world couldn't soften the constant blows. Rob and I were educated, employed, and in a relationship. All signs pointed to getting everything we were ever supposed to want. I was contemplating all this, as one does, when Rob called me from work sounding very excited.

"Twenty-two hundred," he said by way of hello.

"Huh?" *Had he finally figured out how much it would cost to hire a hitman to kill Sallie Mae?*

"That's how much the Brighton School costs—per month."

A new posh preschool was being built blocks away from Rob's office building, and when we were especially drunk, we liked to imagine sending our make-believe kids there with our stockpile of Monopoly money.

"U.S. dollar bucks?" I asked, hoping to clarify.

"Yep."

"Fuck."

"I know."

What we both knew was that, despite not being homeless teenagers, we still weren't ready to take the plunge called pregnancy, because we'd just gotten to the point in the plot where taking care of ourselves was no longer a Herculean effort. By thirtysomething we sort of knew what we were doing—or at least we thought we knew—and no one wanted to have to memorize a new playbook.

Without realizing, I'd done exactly what so many of my happily married friends (and one homeless man) told me I would. I could count on my fingers and toes how many ways I wanted to violently murder folks who had said, "When you stop looking, you'll find him." But I had to admit that they were right. And that pissed me off. So you mean all that longing and daydreaming for Mr. Right was pointless? All I had to do was not die long enough for him to show up? At brunch? Fuck you, universe! After I came up for air from a string of horrible relationships, Rob was waiting with a towel. Thing is, when you finally get what you've waited for—love, commitment, mutual respect—and it comes along so naturally and unexpectedly, it's almost impossible to recognize the gift. Was this thing a boon or a bomb? And where exactly did babies fit in?

You know what happens right after you check all the boxes on your adulting to-do list? College? Career? Legally Permanent Cuddle Partner? Nothing. Absolutely nothing. Actually, no, I'm being unfair, you do get something: more. More empty boxes to be filled, checked, chucked, and stuffed in the back of a closet lest your new husband find out about your casual obsession with vintage lesbian "tribbing" DVDs. More decisions, more responsibilities. More. What happened to "the end" of the fairy tale? Time for the five-hour director's cut.

Fast-forward to our wedding, four years after we met at brunch, and we got more conflicting unsolicited advice about baby-making than personal checks, neither of which we could cash at the bank.

"You guys should wait." "What are you waiting for?!" "This"— said while pointing directly at a tantruming two-year-old—"is not the jam." "Kids are ah-mazing." "Babies are effin' disgusting, why are there so many at this wedding?" "Go stick your uncondomed peen in Helena's vageen right now before the magic goes away!" Okay, no one said that last line, but someone came close. Dangerously close.

When you are weighing the pluses and minuses of creating mini humans, motherhood seems to matter less than getting a baby. The baby's the thing. Your identity as a mother is simply supposed to click. It's supposed to make sense once the baby gets here, which seems ass-backward, right? I am clearly in the chicken before the egg camp. And hatching a plan to have a baby was premature given my own misgivings. Because here's the thing—I wasn't entirely sure I'd be a good mother. Wasn't entirely sure I was good, you know. I mean, I am great. The ABC's of confidence my fourth-grade ballet instructor taught me are basically playing on a loop in my mind all the time. But good? Who knows? Another existential question for you: Is it possible to hate someone for being too good? If so, then I hate Rob with every single twitch of my resting bitch face.

Fine, I'll say it: The man is a better person than me. That's just facts. I don't even feel bad about it—most of the time. He's from the Midwest, a magical land where happy and white people inexplicably say "Hello" as they pass one another on the street and then follow up with a "How are you?" Then—this is the really insane part—they stop and listen for the answer to that obviously rhetorical question. It's fucking nuts.

On top of that, my husband has never once met a random screaming baby he couldn't make laugh, a struggling neighbor whose new IKEA couch he wouldn't help carry up three flights of stairs, an Uber driver whose home country he doesn't want to learn everything about, or a fellow diner whose food didn't look "like something I might like to try."

This is infuriating. More so because it highlights how many strangers I know. Because if there are 318,900,000 people in this country, then there are 318,899,999 people that I do not mess with. I don't have the Rob gene. But what I do have are a very particular set of skills, skills I have acquired over a very long career of walking the gauntlet of street harassers, from L.A. to New York. Skills that make me a nightmare for people like Rob. A flawless RBF. A side-eye that can slice through vibranium. These are skills that Rob promptly ignores when we're out together.

Because we're holding hands, I'm literally being pulled into these stranger-danger situations when all I wanted was a dollar sundae from McDonald's. Really, what drives me nuts is knowing that this whole better-half thing does not in any way, shape, or form apply to me. He's the better one. The good one. I'm just here, smiling awkwardly and salivating over the potential sundae while my husband amiably chats up the guy waiting at the crosswalk with us. And that's also the great thing about it. Rob won't stop holding my hand. He won't let go of me despite the dead weight dragging him down while he's doing the decent thing for the both of us. He's lugging me along whether I like it or not. And I love/hate him for it.

For most normal humans "Cute kid" is a throwaway line—

something you say to besieged new parents as compensation for their pain. *Sorry you're sleep deprived and have shit on your face, but your baby's not fugly. Cheers!* No one means it. Not so for Rob. He not only believes wholeheartedly that your kid is cute but that he must relay this information posthaste, because God forbid you wait in line at Trader Joe's without the singular knowledge that your completely average-looking kid is, according to this complete stranger, cute. See why this whole mom thing was probably not for me? I'm a monster.

Thankfully, "monster" wasn't one of the boxes available to check on the census form.

The census lady showed up at around 11 A.M. on a Tuesday and didn't blink twice at the fact that I was home and half-naked. I answered the door in a ratty T-shirt and a sarong I bought in Spain on one of my last single-lady vacays. She flashed her official badge and asked if she could ask me some questions. I didn't do that thing you do in elementary school and say, "Well, you just did." Instead, I stood there in my holey COLUMBIA CHEER T-shirt and fraying tablecloth for twenty minutes, spilling out the details of my life to a stranger in jeggings.

We'd been married for just under a year, and I'd been feeling like a colossal failure all week. I was off from work, but instead of flying to Havana "before it was ruined" or some other Instagrammable locale that would induce the good kind of jealousy, I was stuck at home scrolling through better people's feeds. Rob's vacation time didn't link up with mine on the calendar, and apparently newly married women weren't allowed to travel alone to Zika territory. So staycation it was. And by *staycation* I don't mean I was a "tourist in my own city." I mean I stayed on the couch and gained an unexplainable five pounds while daydreaming about how much cooler

I'd be with a trust fund or a rich husband. The knock at the door was a welcome break.

"So how much in wages do you make annually," asked the census lady as she stared at the laptop she was carrying from door to door.

"Hmmmm." I was stalling. Only the filthy rich don't know how much money they make a year. "Maybe eighty-eight thousand," I said, trying to sound apologetic, because I was pretty sure not knowing made me sound like an entitled ass. She typed the number in and kept going. What was the highest level of education I'd completed? Master's. Had I been married in the last year? Yep. Did I rent or own? How much was the rent? The answer embarrassed me. Was food included in that number? Food? Huh? No. Did we have any children? Not that I knew of.

"And what was the highest level of education your husband completed?"

"Bachelor's." His income? We still had separate accounts. I gave her a ballpark.

At that she finally looked up from her screen and smiled at me, the blue light giving her face a devilish or angelic sheen, depending on your mood.

"Uh-oh! Power couple."

Wrong. Rob and I had traveled the world; we'd spent a small fortune in rent over the years, blown money on crap we'd eventually put out on the curb, and hosted countless Paperless Post parties featuring me "elegantly carrying around a plate of ribs," as one friend put it. We'd chatted with celebrities at the White House Correspondents' Dinner (including that time Rob formed a nineties-inspired Freak Line with Tatyana Ali and Eric Stonestreet), impressed the black-tie crowd with our well-spokenness at the galas I covered for work, and racked up thousands of likes on silly Facebook declarations of love.

Combined, we made enough money to define us as firmly middle class, but neither one of us felt that way. "Speak for yourself," he told me once after I'd confessed my poor-kid impostor syndrome. I still only put ten dollars at a time on my SmarTrip card because "you can't fucking eat train rides!" Rarely did I ever pay a bill "all the way" even when the money was there. I liked signing in and out of my online bank account throughout the day just to make sure, flinging open a fridge filled with food I didn't feel like cooking, staring at a closet filled with designer-looking clothes I bought on clearance. In my mind the world was always threatening to crash down on our heads, snatching us from the life we were leading and smacking us back to the ones we came from.

Power couple? Those were our friends. Gwen and Sam, who'd just bought a house and talked about planting "privacy trees" in the backyard—like anyone in the suburbs would want to peek through their windows to see them arguing about their kid's organic food. Or my one stay-at-home mom friend from L.A., Lauren, who told me with a straight face that she planned to teach her five-year-old—a well-known asshole, mind you—how to be "a good girl" and do things "the right way, like I did." She meant love, marriage, baby carriage. But I had it on good authority that momming wasn't what Lauren was making it out to be. She'd broken down in tears more than once because her kid wouldn't hug her. Or my friend Tasha, who seemed to hop from one exotic location to the other with her handsome half-Asian husband in tow. Turns out she'd asked him for a divorce twice in the two years since their expensive-ass wedding. These were the alleged power couples. The marrieds who'd made it. While in my big-girl brain I knew that these people didn't have the cheat code, when it came to babies my lizard brain went into fight-or-flight mode. "You guys ready?" asked one of my aunts hopefully during a visit back home to L.A. We'd been running lines on the pros and cons of parenthood by then. No one was truly ready for kids, according to everyone. The idea that some parents had a secret password was just that—an idea. A false perception your mind creates to make sense of the endless horizon. The folks running ahead of you must know what's coming, that's why they're out front and you're bringing up the rear. I didn't have the lung capacity to be running like that. As my aunt waited for a reply I just sighed, too exhausted to tell her the truth.

What did we do before Google? How did we get to the bottom of unknowable questions like "Am I pregnant?" "What do these sore boobs mean?" "Can I eat this can of anchovies if I'm maybe probably with child?" And "Okay, how much is a pregnancy test because I only have twenty dollars in my checking account and payday ain't till Friday?"

I found out I was with child after an epic two weeks of drinking that impressed even me, and I once flipped five dollars into a liquor-induced blackout in college. Cognac was involved. First Rob and I went to Irvington, Virginia, which is exactly as country as it sounds, to celebrate our first anniversary with a wine-soaked weekend. Then, as soon as we got back, I spent the day drinking with my sister-in-law and my cousin-in-law, confessing over champagne how freaked out I'd be if I ever got pregnant with twins. "Not that we're trying or anything!" Because we weren't "trying." We were just not *not* trying. After five years together and no "scares," I was pretty sure it'd take more than a well-timed oopsie to get things going in there. I was misinformed.

Also, I fucking knew better. I'd gotten pregnant my sophomore year at Columbia and pretty much spent the next sixteen years being terrified. "Gotten pregnant" sounds passive. I actively participated and, as so often happens, was left holding my wet panties in the end. I didn't have that potential baby despite my mother's

previous promise that she'd happily raise a grandchild while I finished school, because that whole scenario sounded so Afterschool
Special. There was no question in my mind that that "baby" wasn't
my baby—at least not yet. There were zero regrets when I walked
out of the Planned Parenthood several subway stops away near
NYU and was decidedly unpregnant. But no regrets doesn't mean
no effect. That five-week pregnancy did what it did.

"You'd have like fifty thousand abortions before you did what I
did." This is Sof, my best friend since grad school, drunkenly giving
me her take on my baby prospects without knowing that I was in
fact knocked up. What Sof did was have a baby on her own in her
thirties. Something that I couldn't see myself doing when I was
nineteen because as the child of a single mom I knew firsthand how
thankless that job was. Who does that on purpose? Sof might have
gotten her math wrong—fifty thousand?—but damned if she
wasn't at least partially right. My plan, even if I didn't know it, was
to do it all "the right way." At least on the second take.

According to the rule book only I was studying, I couldn't afford
to throw away all the good bullet points hoarded throughout my
twenties and thirties (degreed-up from my feet up, gainfully
employed, fallen in love with a marriageable man not in jail or on
the DL) on a pregnancy I could've had sophomore year. That was a
fucked-up way to look at it, but there you go. White privilege is
being able to have a baby daddy sans judgment. It's being able to
say "baby daddy" ironically. Like eating watermelon with a pinch of
salt, I'd never do that in mixed company. It didn't matter how many
achievements I had socked away in the success savings account; an
unplanned and out-of-wedlock baby would have zeroed me out.
Matter of fact, it would have probably pushed me into negative. So
before Rob and I got hitched, babies weren't just scary, they were a
nonstarter. How insane is that? How sexist, racist, limiting, and
almost entirely self-imposed? I was the wild and unfathered daugh-

ter of a pot-smoking lesbian hippie; how the hell did I become so
conservative and judgmental? No, I wouldn't do what Sofia did in
fifty thousand years because I wasn't brave enough.

This could be why, when I finally did get pregnant, after years of
avoiding it like the plague it was, I could hardly believe it. Was I
happy about it? Yes? Was I still terrified, despite the ring on my
finger and the direct deposits to my checking account every two
weeks? Yep. A baby—even one sorta planned and sometimes dreamt
about—was still the Boogie Man. That's why I spent an entire week
being pregnant alone. The plan was to wait to tell Rob until I was
absolutely certain this wasn't a fever dream. Every morning I'd go to
the bathroom bracing myself for the bloody square of toilet paper
that never came. Almost immediately I could tell the difference
between being pregnant now and my first accidental insemination.
For one, I was a decade and a half older. I'm not sure if it was time's
toll on my foggy memory or the mileage it took on my body, but
damn if I wasn't exhausted. Barely a month into this thing and
already I wanted to sleep all day, waking up only to shove giant
bowls of pasta into my gaping maw. The first time, I don't remember feeling any different at all. Maybe the crippling shame and
anxiety overpowered all else. Or maybe now I was just old AF, and
my uterus was like, "Bitch, didn't we try to do this almost two
decades ago?" Rude.

What was even more offensive was the fact that Rob hadn't
noticed a thing. When I took a two-hour nap on a Saturday immediately after making breakfast, instead of getting the hint, he just
goes, "What's wrong with you?" After grabbing an overflowing
mound of my previously handful-sized tits he goes, "Wow. That's
what I'm talking about." As if he had prayed for them the night
before. When I asked for crackers in the middle of the night while
practically dry-heaving, he goes, "Fatty." And I ate them silently
seething.

Being secret pregnant is the worst, especially when there's someone who should be settling into their new role as your personal
slave. I couldn't wait for the turnabout when I dramatically revealed,
"I've been pregnant this whole time, ass-face! Now put some pants
on and go get me an anchovy pizza!" That was another clue he'd
missed. My new obsession with anchovies. Rob's reaction: "I can't
wait for you to get over this."

Then I told him, already hopped up on my own self-righteousness,
with a special dinner and a personalized poem with the end line,
"You're going to be a daddy!" Do you know the first thing out of
that man's mouth was, "Yeah, I knew this whole time"? You mean
to tell me I was "hiding" all week for nothing? Turns out Rob had
peeped me checking my period app. He'd just been playing along
for my sake, waiting for me to "come to grips with it." Was that
what I had been doing for the past seven days? Coming to grips
with the potential new me, the mom me? Probably. The fact that
Rob figured that out before I did made me love-hate him even
more. How dare he jack up the emotional IQ in this motherfucker!
Thank God, though, because if I'm honest, it'd been years of running and hiding from the vampire zombie wolves. I was beat. Might
as well remove the barricade at the door and join the horde.

CHAPTER 3

Secret White Meetings

It was deep winter, and I was deeply pregnant and therefore subject to both regular old vagina-specific street harassment *and* bump-specific street harassment, which sounded a lot like creepy advice from that one high school gym teacher all the sweaty girls knew to avoid: "Hey heeeey, that belly's looking ready to *pop*, girl!" "Is it twins?" "You know sex is good for the baby, right?" That last one was shouted at me from across the street by a woman pushing a grocery cart about a mile from the nearest store. I was like a Black whale riding a bicycle through the desert; folks couldn't help but point and yell. But despite the lurking dangers of the outside, I insisted on walking the mile and a half to my office each nippy morning, getting the baby girl inside me primed for what was coming.

It was on these daily wobbles to work that I first discovered "the Infantry," the pack of mommies and babies migrating down our block. Moments after stepping out of our building and onto the street I was immediately met with a flock of jumbo strollers flying by in the opposite direction. They parted around me as if I were a tree and they an unstoppable stampede pounding past in a cloud of dust and coos. Twisting around as much as the basketball lashed to my middle would allow, I watched as this band of mothers expertly rolled through the iron gates of the Episcopal church on the corner in a beautifully choreographed V-formation, disappearing inside to do God knows what. Was this always a thing? How was I just now seeing it? No real surprise there, actually. I'd reached the level of pregnancy in which everything comes up babies. It's like wherever you look there are swollen women and human offspring—suddenly the blackout curtain of singledom is ripped away and instantly there's a spotlight on the fact that procreation is constant, not just a rare condition exclusive to you alone.

Every morning there they were, marching up Second Street for another illicit rendezvous. I stayed the course, positioning my puffed-up body directly in the line of fire to better catch an inkling of their purpose on the wind. Maybe I'd overhear one of the moms slip up about their plot to take over the world. Because what the hell were they doing with those babies in that church every morning? Praying? Human sacrifice? Talking about me? Wait, did I mention that they were all white? Because they were—at least from my vantage point from the outside looking in and feeling left out. It was becoming increasingly apparent that most everything in our neighborhood that related to parents, babies, adulting, home-buying, the farmer's market, renovations, neighborhood clean-ups—and just, you know, living—was dominated by white people. It was stifling, but weirdly motivating, forcing me off the couch and out of my comfort zone. Because I wasn't going to let them have more.

Barely one month past the minefield known as my first trimester, a cartoon wolf named Donald Trump was elected president. Like most sentient beings, I had my mouth all ready for Hillary Clinton. During those early "secret pregnant" months—when only you and a handful of people know—I spent as much time fantasizing about Clinton's inauguration as I did the baby's face. Picturing myself frigid and huge, bumping into other human Otter Pops on the Mall while screaming *"Yassss! Bitch!!!"* after every history-making line of Madam President's address until my lungs gave out and the political mosh pit was forced to crowd-surf me to safety. Did you know that if you forward your baby's birth announcement to the White House, they'll send back an official note of congratulations from the president? In the mail? Like pioneer times? It's the bougiest, most D.C. shit ever (and we have a framed note on expensive cardstock from the Obamas on the occasion of our wedding, thank you very much).

The mental orgasm from the mere possibility of a "Welcome to the world!" message from Hillary hanging in my daughter's nursery nearly sent me into preterm labor. My imaginary *MTV Cribs* episode would go like this: *Oh, hi there. This is where the magic happens! These are her many leather-bound board books. Her handmade mahogany toys. Oh, and over here is a framed invitation from President Hillary Rodham Clinton to join the White House Infant Council.* I could not fucking wait. But nope! You make plans and middle America laughs.

The night we all lost, I went to bed at grandma o'clock, because pregnant. The baby had been sucking away my energy the entire day, making it impossible to keep my eyes open at work, much less stay up all night watching election results roll in with Rob. CNN might as well have been a sound machine. Clinton was up and then I was out. Around 2 A.M. Rob shook me with a violence I'd now describe as tender, like a giant trying clumsily not to bruise an ant.

"Babe. Babe! Wake up," he whisper-screamed.

"What? What!" I replied, assuming we were either being robbed or the Rapture was under way. Looking back, it sort of was.

"Donald Trump is the president of the goddamned United States." Rob delivered this matter-of-factly.

My face froze in an ugly Kabuki mask of angry disbelief that one would assume was due to the gathering political shit storm. But really, it was two hours past midnight, and I was tired.

"Okay," I sighed heavily before rolling to my other side because the internet said lying on one's back was a death sentence for the baby. "I'm sleep, though." But I wasn't. My mind was racing. Immediately the implications of raising a Black child in a world that had no qualms about wearing its racism on its sleeve came crashing down on my middle. Just a week before, we'd found out our baby was a girl. Rob let the patriarchy get the best of him for maybe half a second before he fixed his face, quickly masking any lingering disappointment with enthusiasm. I, on the other hand, couldn't be bothered with political correctness. I burst into psycho, laughing tears.

"I didn't know you wanted a girl," he said in the cramped office, rubbing my back as I ugly cried.

"I didn't. I mean. I don't. I mean I didn't know either," I hiccupped in between happy sobs. It was the truth. I didn't know I wanted a girl. But deep down, who wouldn't? My husband was six foot four, Black as all the things, with a bass that broke hearts in half. How could I not want more of that out in the world? Also, how could I? Boys that would one day look like Rob were under attack, cut down before their chubby cheeks chiseled. Girls were no cakewalk either, but at least I had an inkling of how to mother their struggle. Those tears in the doctor's office were less about rejoicing than they were relief. And yet here we were a week later on election night with a pussy-grabbing president. The hits just wouldn't stop coming. I might as well have been sleeping on my back.

Add to that the fact that, at the time, Rob and I were living in a

formerly racist elementary school in one the most rapidly gentrifying zip codes in the country. Our converted condo building had
once been the white school of our previously segregated neighborhood. The building felt cool and hipster until you thought about
the Ghosts of Jim Crow Past lurking throughout the classrooms-
cum-open-concept-kitchens. My great-grandmother Nonny once
warned me never to go to a funeral pregnant lest the dead person
take the baby with it to the spirit world—or, worse, the baby comes
out looking like whomever's in the casket. But what about the
ghosts we can't shun? The apparitions you can't avoid?

The Infantry was unavoidable. Every morning, there it was.
Smacking me in the face with its supremacist punctuality. No rain,
sleet, or whatever Washington pretends is snow could stop these
moms from marching down the sidewalk en masse, like they owned
it—because they did. Watching them move through the world so
uninhibited shuffled something in me as sure as the baby had
squished my organs. It was decided. Me and the bump weren't
going to give another inch, not on the sidewalk, not in line at the
Ethiopian bodega, not with whatever was going on at that church.
We would not be moved! But let's not get wild, y'all. I was hardly
the Rosa Parks of parenting, but I would get to the bottom of a
common occurrence Black folks are all too familiar with—the
Secret White Meeting.

Here's the deal: Black women, we keep our heads on a swivel.
We stay ready, constantly on high alert to protect ourselves from
physical violence, emotional harm, career backstabbing, and nasty
potato salad. Chief among the many potholes marring our path is
the Secret White Meeting. Never heard of it? Probably because
you've never had to put a name to your own exclusion. Welcome to
America. Basically, the Secret White Meeting is exactly what it
sounds like. It can be an actual formal meeting held in that glass
conference room at work, making your Black-ass absence all the

more obvious. Or it can be a hushed conversation in the ladies'
room between two white colleagues who then have the nerve to
give *you* the side-eye as you're exiting a stall, as if your very existence
is trespassing on theirs. Sometimes it's just a feeling—a viscous
something in the air—that there's an "Open sesame!" floating
around and you can't catch it. Or perhaps a white moms' meetup at
the Black church on the corner.

One of the first mainstream cultural references to the Secret
White Meeting, a centuries-old phenomenon, appears in Issa Rae's
HBO juggernaut *Insecure*. In the comedy's first season, Issa's then
perpetually awkward and Black character (also named Issa) is struggling in a dead-end job but trying to make the most of it. Instead
of offering actual support, her white colleagues pick apart a big
project she's planning. Issa overhears them shit-talking her in the
break room, and when she busts in to catch them in the act, they're
all smiles. (Another facet of Secret White Meetings is that we've been
gaslit into thinking they are all in our heads.)

"Issa, hey," one co-worker chimes in with a fake smile. A telltale
sign.

"How are you doing," one of the offenders offers in the same
singsong. "Are you stressed? I would be *so* stressed. Like *so stressed*."

Issa just stands there and makes everyone uncomfortable with a
"Say it to my face" stare. But her tiny victory is short-lived. Later,
she finds out that the break-room backstabbing wasn't all: There
were some "concerns" raised via email too, and it's safe to say she
wasn't cc'd.

"They're having secret white meetings, and they're sending secret
white emails," Issa narrates to her boyfriend that night, releasing all
the pent-up frustration of not knowing but knowing, you know?

The early morning church meetups were that. I just knew they
were.

A Secret White Meeting that I had hitherto known absolutely

nothing about somehow offended every fiber of my being—and my unborn child's. How *dare* these complete strangers conduct some clandestine skull-and-baby-bones-type shit without at least posting flyers about it outside the Ethiopian bodega? Could I have just asked one of the moms where they were going? Sure, whatever, maybe. But instead, I seethed for weeks, daydreaming about all the things these women could've possibly been doing with those babies in the basement of St. James when my Google search brought up nothing.

"What if it's a daycare!" I whispered one morning while on the phone with Rob, having just witnessed the Infantry marching through the gates.

"Okay."

"It's right across the street! A freaking daycare we know nothing about! I'm going to do some recon."

"Ummmhmmm."

"Are you listening? Do you realize we need someone to take care of this baby that's about to drop?"

"She's not an album," Rob replies.

"Right! She has zero ROI. We need help."

"Want me to go over there and find out?"

"No no no no. You'll ruin it," I said, without being super clear on what exactly my husband might ruin—the mystery, the suspense, my favorite guessing game. We went around like that for days until finally I cracked the code (read: I just asked one of the moms one morning). What had been keeping me silent for so long was another awkward aspect of the Secret White Meeting—not wanting to admit that you're on the outside looking in. I mean, that was quite literally what was happening. But I had to pretend as if I knew exactly what was going on in there while trying to figure out what was going in there. See? Easy. It was a losing game with made-up sides. Basically, the concept of race in a nutshell. Summoning up

the courage—*pfft*, please—wasn't the problem. It was about vulnerability (because that's what lack of knowledge is in the end, right?).
Revealing my ignorance to women I've learned through my own
experiences—and those deep ones swimming in my blood—that
you should never under any circumstances be vulnerable with was
dangerous. This is what it's like being a Black mom surrounded—
nothing is as simple as it should be. Me? Ask who? A what? Why
not admit to the whole damn world that I had no clue what I was
doing with this baby in my belly and just hand my phone over with
Child and Family Services already dialed.

When I finally rolled up on a woman with a messy bun pushing
her jogging stroller up the bricked sidewalk, I was filled to bursting
with my personal crusade to put an end to Secret White Meetings
once and for all—or at least for me.

"Hey," I politely shouted while ever so slightly opening my XL
parka to reveal the bump, "what's going on in there?" The plan had
been to sound more curious than accusatory, but too late. *Tell me or
else, lady!*

"Oh! Hello? Yeah, it's just Mister Mike's," she answered offhand-
edly, not even slowing her stride. Great. Another moat. I tried not
to let it show on my face, but I had no clue who that was. But my
mind, failing to climb out of the gutter, immediately went to the
dry-humping thongs of *Magic Mike,* and I knew full well these hoes
weren't training stripper tots.

"I'm sorry, who?"

She stopped to take me in. With one hand on her stroller and
the other on the gate, she said, "Ah, right! Right. Mister Mike's
Music class. He does them all over the city. This is our neighborhood's spot." And just like that I was initiated into the Infantry. I
joined the cult of classes as soon as Sally was big enough to be
toted, hatless, outside without the disapproving pursed lips of older
Black women everywhere. Wait, no, our neighbor lady Miss Carole

always ever so slightly (but pointedly) shook her head when she saw me packing up the tiny human. *Keep that baby in the house,* I knew she was ordering me in her head, but I'd just wave and walk on. And the two of us would head into another full week of wholly unnecessary newborn finishing school.

At the top of my list was Mister Mike's, of course, which I learned from Messy Bun Mom was music development that laid the necessary foundation of melody and rhythm integral to formal training later in life. Also, it was $250 for ten classes but the newborn course was "no cost"—similar to how a crack dealer gives away freebies to ensure the clientele stays hooked. Sign us up!

In no time my phone was constantly abuzz with reminders of the many, many ways in which I was supposed to be "pouring into" my child. You'd think the kid would be full after one, maybe two classes. But nope. Never. Once I knew that class on class on class was what all the *other* moms were doing with their kids on a weekday morning, there was no way I'd be caught binging another episode of *Game of Thrones* at 10 A.M.—at least not while quality baby brains were developing with the help of experts somewhere out in the world.

It was at Mister Mike's, in a class led by a woman named Miss Linda, who had the voice of a frustrated opera singer, that I came face-to-face and toe-to-toe with the women I'd been creeping on, criticizing, and plotting to infiltrate for months. These were other first-timers, whom I recognized from the Facebook group, that disastrous crybaby matinée, and the hangout tree in Crispus Attucks Park—Meghan, Leah, Carly, Mira, et al. We were all technically Mamas, of course, having been referred to the larger Facebook group while pregnant and thirsty for support, and then getting drunk off the collective Kool-Aid. It was music class on Tuesdays and on Wednesdays baby yoga with Rachel, who reminded us at the close of every thirty-minute jam session of "Namaste Yay!" that we should "hang out afterward and chat." Getting to know other moms was the whole point—because yoga for a seven-week-old, seriously?

I felt awkward and out-of-place at first. I was a new mom, the only Black girl, and I was obviously too cool for these people, right? On the first day of music class Sally and I arrived early so as not to miss any secret goings-on (and also because, as the only Black people, showing up late was not a good look). The Infantry arrived minutes later, and as always, the moms seemed to know one another already, like there was an invite-only pregame beforehand. I recognized Meghan immediately. Thinking us sorta kinda friends in the way Facebook tricks you into false intimacy, I quarter-smiled her way. She was cordial but not cloying, offering a halfhearted wave that said something like, *Do we know each other? Maybe?* We didn't, of course. Even after recognizing most of the women in the basement rumpus room that served as Miss Linda's stage, I still felt alone. Of course I did. We didn't truly know each other yet and had little in common beyond the babies. And despite my gung-ho approach to the cult of class, that didn't change the fact that the whole idea of class for babies is dumb. But remember: Secret White Meeting. I couldn't bow out lest Sally be left in the dust while the rest of these kids babbled along to "The Wheels on the Bus" and barreled *Speed*-style toward bright futures.

So there I was following Miss Linda's careful instructions to "la, la, laaaaaaa" in the baby's direction, clang cymbals over her face, and tickle her nose with silk no matter how silly it made me feel. Plus, Sally actually giggled and, dare I say, sang a note or two, instantly melting my too-cool-for-school heart. The kid was laughing ahead of schedule, and I was in pants before 4 P.M. This couldn't be all bad despite the cringeworthy moments that made me question my entire mothering philosophy—which at this point was based on what, exactly? Keeping up? Getting ahead? Staying on beat?

Case in point: One of the babies' favorite activities during music was to watch the grown-ups "dance" around like idiots while billowing a giant Technicolor parachute over their tiny heads. I say "dance," but that is absolutely not what the eight of us were doing. Stereotypes are bad, guys. Full stop. But also, like, a little bit true sometimes? Let's just say the rhythm of our rainbow circle was severely lacking in syncopation. The two-step might as well have been the tango. It's never looked so complicated. The term "circle jerk" took on new meaning. That's what we looked like, a bunch of jerks in a circle. And there I was singing "Head, Shoulders, Knees, and Toes" to Sally in my best Mariah vibrato while trying not to bump into the mom to my right, who was doing God only knows with her feet. But it's near impossible to stay on beat in a mosh pit of folks who can't find it to save their lives. That's a metaphor for something.

The road from skeptic to zealot was so seemingly smooth I barely noticed the sharp turn. The girl who in her blissful twenties formed an informal committee dubbed "Keep U Street Black!!!" for the sole purpose of "Black-people bombing" every new hipster joint north of Fourteenth Street was now bogarting the good tables at the corner coffee shop in the middle of the afternoon with a bunch of moms popping their nipples out with abandon. I remember this one time—back when the idea of having children was akin to contracting an STD—my sorority sister Deja and I were disgusted to the point of gagging after a woman with an impossibly long brunette ponytail sat at the table next to us in a restaurant and let her two-year-old reach into her blouse, pull out a nip, and go to town. Did I mention this tiny Renaissance adult had just taken a bite of spring greens? Was expertly using a fork? We were appalled. The nerve of these people moving onto the block and brandishing their boobs like they were on the menu.

"Salad! The baby was eating salad," we yelled when recounting the story to anyone who'd listen. "White people," we concluded, shaking our heads in unison (and on beat, I might add).

Flash-forward twenty years later and Deja was living in Miami, "extended breastfeeding" all four (yes, four, like a TLC reality show) of her kids in some vegan hot spot. While I was in D.C. diving into the finer points of "power pumping" with Carly, a Bloomingdale Mama whose preemie son refused the boob, leaving his mom— a woman determined, with spindly arms and telltale dark circles under her eyes—to pump every hour on the hour twelve hours a day to make sure he got his fill of the good stuff.

"I just . . . I don't know how long I can keep this up," Carly admitted over an everything bagel and chai latte one morning as the group of us sat stroller to stroller shushing babies. She was exhausted and embarrassed and barely holding on.

"Do you even want to?" I asked, suddenly profound after seven weeks. She wasn't sure. "It's tough," I said. "Because you'll have to mourn whatever version of yourself you thought was *the* version before you let that shit go." Carly looked down at her baby, a fussy ball of strawberry blond, and nodded softly. Who was I? Where did this sudden wisdom, call it maturity, come from? Was being around "those fucking girls," as my pal Sofia called them, actually bringing out some new version of me?

Slowly but surely, they started to grow on me. Like when Mira's mother, a tiny lion with permanent mascara and a gymnast's thighs who, like all grandmas these days, wanted to be called something other than "Grandma," started showing up to Mister Mike's and putting us all to shame. Mimi was Miss Linda's star student—setting up the tiny instruments before class, laying out the rainbow parachute, jumping up from the floor and plopping down again without groaning, while making sure Mira's baby never let a full cry escape her lips.

"Man," I whispered to Mira one day during a diaper break after Mimi had uncharacteristically unhanded her granddaughter for five minutes, "your mom is a freaking iPhone. Mine would never."

She rolled her eyes. "I know. This is, like, her stage." Turns out this Mimi was a "show grandma," one of those ladies who live for their grandbabies in exuberant public fits and bursts. She'd be back home in Indiana in a week or so and Mira would get her house back without the manic flurry of cleaning, cooking, and judgment. "I cannot wait," she said. I knew the feeling. When my own mother showed up at one of Sally's music classes, she regaled us all with the screechy soprano she'd perfected at Citizens of Zion Missionary Baptist Church of Watts and the drumming-circle skills of her lesbian sweat lodge days. Stage indeed. I was annoyed but hardly alone.

But just as I was getting comfortable, the bar that only I could see was raised ever so slightly yet again. Sally, in my completely unbiased opinion, was a goddamn rock star. Baby girl was Gerber cute. Her laugh birthed a gazillion fairies. Her smile was legend. But she was slow to roll over. So obviously I was failing this child in some deep-seated way. All the books said she would get the hang of it by four months. It'd been seventeen weeks. We had a problem. And guess whose baby didn't. Meghan's. Always Meghan.

The group of us were basking in the "class is over" afterglow when I heard them—the shrieks.

"Ahhhh, ahhhh, ahhhh," chimed Carly and the rest of the circle as they cheered on Meghan's daughter, who was rocking from left to right like a dinghy on the high seas until *boom* she'd rolled over.

On. Both. Sides. I clapped along with the chorus while silently sinking into internal panic mode.

"Wow, I can't believe she did that already. Both sides? Wow," I said by way of congratulations—as if Meghan herself had just won the hundred-meter dash at the Olympics—because at this point in the mothering journey all your baby's accomplishments are yours for the taking. What your offspring does or doesn't do is a direct reflection on you and your abilities, no one else's—not the actual baby's, not your husband's, not the system. You. "Sally's still just thinking about it."

"Oh, don't worry," replied Meghan in an offhanded tone that I believe was meant to be reassuring but, filtered through my Black Mama universal translator, was condescending as hell. "She'll get there. Remember, you can't compare them."

Bitch, what? The hell I can't.

In any other context, Meghan's "advice" would have been harmless. Helpful even. Of course you shouldn't comparison-shop your babies, especially as a frazzled new mom who agonizes over every developmental milestone not yet reached (rolling over, laughing, producing perfectly molded poops). The unchecked list is not only a confirmation of your abysmal parenting skills, but also a clear indication of your child's inevitable future as a low-functioning adult. Obviously, we shouldn't compare them. It's a losing game. Plus, every baby is different; they all go at their own pace; childhood isn't a race, blah, bladdity, blah, blah, blah.

But in this context, with me being the only Black mom in the room, a statement like Meghan's had a subtext so blazing it was written in neon. Why would *my* baby not measure up? Why would I, out of all the other mothers in this room, need to temper my expectations? Well, one, because I was being a nut, but that's beside the point. Race is never invisible, especially when it's being actively ignored. Was she being racist? Of course not. If anything, she was offering space on the raft to another drowning mom. But was the moment filled with racial implications for me? Absolutely.

Before the baby I would hardly have described myself as a competitive person. Not because I lack confidence. Quite the contrary. My logic goes like this: I already know I'll beat you, so why sweat my press out sprinting around the track in the first place? I'd rather stand behind the finish line sipping champagne and golf-clapping for the worn-out runners barreling through the cheap tape, satisfied in the singular knowledge that I would've ate everybody up if only I were hungry enough. But *baaaaabay,* does a baby change things. Now, that same practiced narcissism—honed through decades of only-child navel-gazing—could very well be described in some circles as neglect. There was only one reasonable response to Meghan's kind counsel: doubling down.

Through my new-mommy fog, it became clear to me that Sally *needed* this more than ever. She needed the socialization, the stimulation, the hand-eye coordination, the self-soothing techniques, the exposure. All of it. She needed not just to win but to beat these other kids. So we classed the fuck up. Added to the Google Calendar dance parties at the public library, African drumming, story time plus modern art at the Smithsonian, and the rest of the board-book course catalog that makes up the daily lives of women on maternity leave. It was insane. There was no way around that, and there was no way I wasn't signing up for every last course. Every. Last. One.

If this particular brand of parenting sounds over-the-top, that's because it is. But it's also not new. There's even a name for it— "intensive mothering," because, well, it's always the mother, isn't it? Trust Rob was not agonizing over whether Sally was babbling the appropriate number of consonant sounds at six months.

First coined in the late nineties by sociologist Sharon Hays, "intensive mothering" is exactly what is sounds like, mothering as an active verb, mothering as competition. It's a parenting philosophy born of the middle-class economic anxiety of the eighties and nineties. Taking root in the soil of Reaganomics and growing up a trellis made of discarded bootstraps, intensive mothering firmly places child-rearing in the hands of the career woman. She alone could fix it. Her "job," on top of the backbreaking work of breaking glass ceilings, was to hold the umbrella for her kid while dragging said kid up the ladder too. Its exhausted devotees define "good parenting" as "child-centered, expert-guided, emotionally absorbing, labor-intensive, and financially expensive."

This is when folks went from yelling, "Go play outside!" at their kids to scheduling playdates. These are the moms who look at an unplanned Saturday like iceberg lettuce—empty calories. In the nineties, motherhood became more individualized, self-reliant, and self-governed. Sounds lonely, right? With the rise of the "working mom," motherhood became about raising the perfect child and the practice of "mothering" became an investment in their future success. *Who's going to make it? Not my friend's kid, my kid.* What is this, *The Hunger Games?* Yes, yes, it is. And in the decades since Hays first put her finger on the extreme pressure working middle-class mothers were under, we've only gone more bonkers. Hello helicopter, lawnmower, snowplow, bulldozer, elephant, tiger, and dolphin parenting.

But as the successful adult daughter of a former flower child with limited financial resources who believed in free-range kids before there was a buzzword for it, shouldn't I have known better? Like most latchkey kids, I was raised by an Avengers-style team of strict aunts, indifferent uncles, cool older cousins, and judgy church ladies, on top of my own actual mother. Oh, and also TV. No one was stressing over Gymboree waitlists. For them, raising children was an organic-community-garden-style endeavor.

There's a specificity to African American parenting in this country. Around the same time intensive mothering was making its prime-time debut, groundbreaking theorist and OG Black feminist Patricia Hill Collins put the spotlight on Black mothering, othermothering, and community mothering. She placed child-rearing in a racial and ethnic context separate from the mainstream definition, which up to then was chiefly concerned with the white, the middle-class, the college-educated. Dr. Collins's point was that *we* did things differently for good reason and *different* didn't mean "less than." After centuries of having their families and homes violently torn apart, free Black mothers defended those spaces as sacrosanct. Rather than being collectively oppressed by their domesticity (like the frustrated women of Betty Friedan's *The Feminine Mystique*), Black women saw their status as mothers as nothing short of revolutionary.

It was this brand of Black mother love that author and publisher Denene Millner sought to highlight with her acclaimed online parenting community, MyBrownBaby.com. It was a love that was familiar to Millner, a daughter of working-class parents and Brooklyn. Her mother spent long days at a factory. PTA meetings weren't in her purview. She didn't have time to "do all the crazy shit we do now for our kids," said Millner in a phone interview with yours truly. And yet, Millner felt loved-on hard, highly valued, and fiercely protected by a tight-knit community. It's the same way I felt as a kid.

"That kind of community-based parenting was rooted in Black culture. You had to stick close to one another and hold each other in regard because nobody else was going to do it. I don't know if they sat around and thought about their identities as mothers—their philosophies. But just because they didn't have the language for it doesn't mean they didn't take the job seriously. They all regarded us in the same way—as deeply important to them, the human beings that they wanted to see thrive. They just didn't say it the way that we say it. They weren't beating their chests and saying, 'I'm a mother.' They had other stuff they had to do," continued Millner, whose children's book imprint at Simon & Schuster centers the everyday joy of Black girls and boys.

When raising her own two daughters, Millner went all in, absorbing the intense love she felt from her community child-rearing and adding to the mix her own professional badass Black working mom ethos. It was the 2000s and "helicopter parenting" was the philosophy du jour. "That wasn't just a white-women thing, that was an every mother thing. We just started saying out loud what our mothers had practiced," explained Millner, who considered her own mother's parenting to be just as laser-focused, if not as minutiae-obsessed, as the rich white helicopter moms being touted as the "it" moms of the new millennium. Black mothers had been on that. Millner and her close cohort of mom friends—connected African American media professionals raising kids in fast-paced New York City—were determined to make sure their kids were doing all the same things the other kids were doing.

"Our kids weren't going to be left behind through lack of effort on our part. It wouldn't be because we weren't paying attention," she said. Her mom was the same way. What she wasn't doing was baking two dozen brownies for the bake sale or blowing billable hours as a "room mom." But "she was there when it was necessary. To check people when they forgot who her daughter was. She was the closer," said Denene, painting a picture of her mother that looked exactly like my mom, like my grandmommy. Women who weren't rich or white but who took parenting very seriously without letting it consume them.

I know all of this. I know that mothering as a Black woman means resilience, magic, and grit. That it doesn't require anything fancy to be phenomenal. That it stares into the sharp jaws of a many-headed beast—racism, sexism, classism, ableism, all the isms—and persists with a tone, a look only we possess. I know that, as my mother says, "it doesn't take much" but that it really does, just not the kind of "much" the mainstream measures. I *know* this. And yet. And yet. There I was bicycling my baby's legs in yoga and bouncing her to the beat at Mister Mike's. Doing all the things these *other* moms were doing even when I knew it was hardly the one and only way. Or even the right way. Was I infiltrating the Secret White Meeting or being indoctrinated?

"Well-educated professional women tend very much to be engaged in intensive mothering and that often crosses race lines," explained motherhood scholar Lynn O'Brien Hallstein over the phone, as I peppered her like a therapist with existential questions about being a Black woman momming in predominantly white spaces. Class, often overlooked, plays a major role in how we parent, said O'Brien Hallstein. Our education leads to socioeconomic privilege, which in turn leads to anxiety over keeping said privilege (you know, the whole "mo' money, mo' problems" ideology) and passing it down to your kids. The cyclone doesn't stop, and it also doesn't skip over our house because we Black in here. We're all caught up in the whirlwind. Not to mention the fact that, in America, the more successful you are, the whiter and whiter the spaces you inhabit become.

"It's hard to resist intensive mothering practices," said O'Brien Hallstein, especially when you're hemmed in on all sides. Being one of the only Black moms in a neighborhood filled with privileged white moms didn't mean—when I didn't see myself reflected in their hysteria—that I'd reject them. Quite the opposite. "You would be pulled much more toward that than pushed away," said O'Brien Hallstein, offering me an ethical escape hatch. She called the mothering I described in our neighborhood—filled with classes, meetups, playdates, and endless debates about wake times—"intensive mothering on steroids." And it's all too easy to get addicted, despite the side effects.

Andrea O'Reilly, founder and publisher of Demeter Press, the first feminist press on motherhood, describes the constant internal mind-looping some mothers of color experience "as a tension between mothering according to their own values and mothering according to the dominant values." And the contemporary dominant values defining "good mothering" include a laundry list of impossibilities no non-robot woman can attain—full-time mothering, children at the center of everything, work on the back burner, and a PhD in parenting philosophies even though mothering should come naturally to anyone with a vagina. It's a 1950s fever dream on twenty-first-century zombie weed.

"The good mother trope has seldom been available to Black women," she told me. The images we see of motherhood, whether on-screen or in our faces every day, have been largely shaped by the "mainstream" culture, so it's no surprise that it's whitewashed. If you immediately thought, *Wait, what about Clair Huxtable? Michelle Obama? That lady from . . .* then my point is proven. Call me when the list gets past a high five in length.

Since its coinage, "intensive mothering" has been viewed as a white concept and identity, but it is increasingly being practiced by upper-middle-class Black mothers, explained O'Reilly. Society just assumes we don't participate in the craziness because it so often lumps race and class together. But Black mothers parent like a motherfucker too. Their efforts just go unseen.

Millner explained, "People just didn't recognize that we were out there because the running narrative was that we were reluctant parents who didn't know how to raise children. I always took issue with the term 'helicopter parenting' as some kind of negative thing. I think that Black women do well when we are watching, because you see what happens to our children when we are not."

"For Black mothers, intensive mothering could be a radical act," said O'Reilly. "Yes, it can be disempowering, but for Black mothers it can also be defiant, because society's telling her the exact opposite. It's political if a Black mother does it." Okay, okay. All right, Andrea. So maybe I *was* the Rosa Parks of parenting.

Annette Lareau, a sociologist who now works at the University of Pennsylvania, identified another aspect of privileged parent problems with the phrase "concerted cultivation." The term is a gardening reference meant to evoke a style of child-rearing in which a methodical approach produces the desired result, like an artfully pruned bonsai tree that grows just so. But the tree is your kid.

This idea resonated during my conversation with Lynn O'Brien Hallstein. "For most contemporary mothers, particularly well-educated mothers who also have socioeconomic privilege, the big worry now is that they have to cultivate their children's lives for success," she said. "So that's what's at the root of all this worry about getting into the right schools, picking the right classes, you know, living in the right neighborhoods. It's also a uniquely American struggle. Because of individualism and the lack of social support and structures, it's really on a family's shoulders to ensure children's success." Now imagine what it's like for a Black mom.

In her book *Unequal Childhoods,* Lareau investigates the divergent ways in which different economic classes parent. Her conclusions make a lot of sense. Parents from working-class backgrounds in general let their kids just be. They didn't hover. They didn't overschedule. They didn't feel the need to constantly entertain their kids or pack every hour with "enrichment." Instead, they saw childhood as a worry-free zone that shouldn't be muddied up with responsibilities or adult-like expectations. There would be plenty of time for that in actual adulthood, which in this group's view was too often filled with unfulfilling work and economic stress. So let them eat cake!

On the other hand, middle-class parents, many of whom had grown up working class and were now occupying a new social status (raises hand), always had adulthood on the brain. The wonder years were less about wonder and more about laying the groundwork. "The middle-class version of adulthood is one that is going to be exciting, pleasant, and varied—where you can actualize your interests and become an individual and do things that are important in the world and be a success," explained Lareau to me in an interview. Man, that sounds nuts when she says it, right? But also exactly what I picture when I spend shower time dreaming up Sally's future wins.

"The idea is that middle-class parents treat their children as if they're a project. They consistently, even relentlessly, work to develop their talents and skills. Their goal in childhood is often exposure," continued Lareau. These parents think, *I don't want them to be Mozart, but I want them to know how to play the piano.* Guilty. By eighteen months Sally—who'd already had a freshman liberal art major's load of music, yoga, and swimming—was on the waitlist for baby and me ballet. I didn't expect homegirl to be Misty Copeland (okay, fine, I did), but she'd at least know how to plié with a proper turnout. Would that skill be helpful down the road? Probably not. But that didn't stop me. Exposure, remember? On top of that, baby girl couldn't just take "regular" ballet. I had to find a Black ballet teacher, preferably one with almond-colored skin and properly moisturized 4c curls. Also, the class had to have at least two other Black girls in it.

Black moms do so much plucking and pruning. The "right school" isn't just one with good test scores, it should also have the right number of Black teachers (and please let some of them be Black men) and not have a track record of disciplining Black children more harshly than their white classmates or of doing Black History Month as an afterthought or twenty-eight days of struggle.

Basically, we do all the white stuff *plus* the Black stuff. A lot has been said about mental labor, invisible work, all the work women do that society ignores. Well, Black moms are doing that and then some. Because for us there's always more to consider as we factor in what "shapes your life profoundly" (that's O'Brien Hallstein again), like everything that happens on the other side of our front door. History, privilege, politics, and family get twisted up together in a knot that can't be undone.

During our conversation, Lareau freely admitted that Black moms were the busiest moms. "They would go through a lot of mental work, constantly scoping out the racial balance of all these organized activities," she said, sounding almost astonished by all the unpaid overtime. When it came to her own research, Lareau agonized over how to frame this additional load placed squarely on the shoulders of Black mothers. Was it something entirely separate or perfectly in line with the concept of concerted cultivation? Should she place it in its own category of mothering or throw it on top of the already unbalanced scale? In the end, Lareau decided on the latter.

"So, there's been a cottage industry trying to prove me wrong about that, that I've downplayed race," said Lareau, referring to the notion that the racial calculations Black moms make on a daily basis should be an issue separated from the mental load of juggling doctors' appointments and soccer practice. "It's unresolved. It's an ongoing debate in the field of sociology."

And also in my head, as I make sure the dolls I buy have the plastic equivalent of kinky hair and the blond girls Sally runs behind on the playground are nice to her. It's another thick layer of "intensive mothering" that makes the mothering harder in these quiet ways only Black mothers understand. A raging battle that doesn't make a sound. Or perhaps it shrieks.

That's another reason Meghan's comment about not comparing our babies got to me. No, we could never compare them. Sure, childhood was a marathon not a sprint. But not for me and mine. Sally was already racing faster than her chubby legs would ever go, like a duck paddling furiously under the water. Those other moms just couldn't see it.

CHAPTER 4

Super Cool Moms

When we got Covid I was too embarrassed to tell anyone—except the Super Cool Moms.

Okay, let me back up. At this point in the story, I now have two daughters, Sally and Robyn. I'd reached the level of motherhood where the intensity had gone from cold-shower shocking to "Oh, this? This is just a Saturday." I'd been a frequent FFPPU poster and sleep-training-advice slanger on the Mamas for nearly three years. Basically, I was a junior in mommy college, over the freshman jitters and pretty confident of my place in the larger hierarchy. My crew ran deep too, made up of all my fellow concerted cultivators who met during our collective new-mom fog and stayed connected despite the stupor. There was even a name for our upper-crust mommy clique—the Super Cool Moms.

Of course, I resisted at first, because, despite getting more comfortable, I was always cautious. But the universe itself seemed to be pushing us together. Approximately twenty months after our freshman orientation as the new moms of Bloomingdale Parenting U, a

handful of us showed up to U2 Toddler Soccer with terrible toddlers and nearly identical baby bumps. And guess who I spied, with
a belly as big as mine, chasing after her own mini Rapinoe? Meghan,
always Meghan. I audibly groaned.

It'd been well over a year and I still hadn't gotten over that "you
can't compare them" comment from baby music class. It was seared
into my brain. Another piece of damning evidence that I would
never really belong and probably didn't want to. So when someone
posted in the Mamas about starting an offshoot group for ladies
birthing babies that fall, and I saw Meghan's name among the likes,
I got angry excited. It was the kind of "mixed feeling" Daniel Tiger
taught Sally (and me) was okay. I knew how crucial a maternity-
leave clique was, but I also never forgot that feeling of being lost
in the crowd. Plus, since having Sally I'd been collecting all sorts
of mom friends—from work Slack groups to random Columbia
alumnae events; heck, I had even helped charter a chapter of Mocha
Moms, a support group created specifically for Black mothers. (Did
I mention I'm a joiner?) But see, how my follow-through is set up,
regularly scheduled meetings with agendas and officer elections and
dues are just . . . above me now.

The women in arm's reach were grab-and-go. Easy and, more
important, in seemingly endless supply. Like most of my mommy
foibles there's a name for this geographical pull—the power of
proximity. Psychologist Susan Pinker gets into it in her book, *The
Village Effect: How Face-to-Face Contact Can Make Us Healthier,
Happier, and Smarter.* In short, people need people. Duh. Bloomingdale just kept calling. We were all so fucking fertile. Resistance was
futile.

Also booze. Much like the beginning of this entire baby saga, in
the end it was the liquor that got me. Someone made the genius
suggestion that we switch up the game a little and meet at our local
pub for early happy hour with the 2.0 babies—and well, there you

go. Deal sealed. We fell into a familiar rhythm, once again becoming more than Facebook comments to one another. During our matched-up maternity leaves we met twice a week, sometimes more, mostly sipping barely alcoholic ciders while nursing new babies and complaining about how insane our toddlers were. I'd finally calmed down enough as a mom—as a Black woman—to just shut up and enjoy my slight buzz.

That's how I got over myself long enough to truly see Meghan for the unmatched type-A mega-mind that she was. The woman had an article, a study, a policy paper handy for every situation. Her endless repository of logistical solutions to everything from daycare drop-offs to get-out-the-vote drives was motivating. I was still too lazy to do more than send virtual high fives, though. Leah's family campouts with two kids under two were aspirational. (Hence the trip to REI that made me feel like a success without ever stepping foot on an actual campground.) Carly's occasional freak-outs over her kid not doing enough "art or whatever" was a reminder to relax (and that my kids needed to do more coloring and shit). Tiffany telling me that irregular bathing for kids was actually good for their health was a warning (nope). Our in-person meetups had once again fallen into a comfortable rhythm; they were an essential part of our lives as Bloomingdale's moms. We discussed the babies but also politics, the women's movement, *Love Is Blind*, and how out of control the housing market was getting. Our weeks together resembled the lazy hazy days of summer camp, where platonic love gets microwaved over deep confessions and contraband candy. We even solidified the pact with the twenty-first-century equivalent of the friendship bracelet, a WhatsApp group called "Super Cool Moms" because we thought of one another that way. Super cool. Don't laugh.

It surprised me at first. How your friends who are moms aren't necessarily your mom friends and how women I used to clown became my confidantes. Our pasts were almost as blank as our babies', leaving it up to us to fill in our stories how we saw fit, piecing together the best-ish versions of ourselves for one another. It's like how you go to college and can rebrand, minus whatever embarrassing thing defined you all through high school. I'd never been anything but a mom to these women, and that was in and of itself freeing. I didn't have to hide from that identity or shrink it down or wave it away with my hand in favor of some better Helena, some other version of me from a zillion years ago without lightning bolts across her stomach. I'd found common ground (if not always cause) with people who knew me without the baggage of Before, despite still being "the only one" in the group.

Which brings up another cool thing about the Super Cool Moms. I was not, in fact, the only one. Not in the most literal sense anyway. I was still the only Black mom, but as the hundreds of women that made up the Mamas simmered down to the more palatable group chat, I started to taste the nuance. They weren't just "not Black." I mean, they weren't Black. But the Super Cool Moms weren't all white either. Tina and Nancy were Korean American. Angie and Priya were Indian American. The racial makeup of this smaller group was more complex than simply Black versus white, although white always seemed to be the default. In my mind's eye I still saw all of them as "white girls," which is a protective thing I think Black women do, lumping all the people not us into one big group so it's easier to avoid. But, man, did Covid kick through some lines in the sand.

More than former strangers, there was a time when we were practically invisible to one another. Before having babies (and then more babies), most of us had been neighbors in name only, looking past one another in silence on First Street while mentally scrolling through a Whole Foods run or imagining that thing you should've said to your husband in that one fight that would've ended patriarchy for good this time. The other body on the sidewalk might as well have been an orange safety cone, annoyingly bright and avoidable by design. Now look at us, clinging to one another like life rafts.

When the pandemic dropped like an anvil on our lives and the world subsequently caved in, WhatsApp was like a flashlight. Meghan, of course, was still our resident know-it-all, and I mean that in the best way possible. Have a question and she had the answer, from ever-changing Covid protocols to fact sheets about the faraway possibility of daycare ever opening again. I asked WhatsApp more questions than Google. Leah, whose boss was Mother Nature, had escaped to the mountains with her twins, husband, and a spry mother-in-law in tow. She sent us dispatches from the woods and, bless her, complained about the free childcare—because no one's life can be that *Little House on the Prairie* perfect. As usual Carly was still pulling all-nighters at her law firm and driving sixteen hours at a clip to get help from her own mom with her son, a singleton who after those early stressful years of what-ifs (what if he doesn't latch, doesn't talk, doesn't who knows?) was now a babbling chubster with too many teeth. Mira, the dark-haired curmudgeon for whom global panics are made, took it all on the chin. No handwringing for her; as soon as daycares opened back up, her kids were going. I took a little bit from each one. I'd quote snippets from threads on the potential vaccine (Dr. Tiffany said it'd be safe), the finale of *Indian Matchmaking* (Nancy was mad I ruined it with my overexcited typing fingers), and the best fancy takeout (Priya voted for Annabelle) to Rob.

"Well, according to the moms . . ." I'd start. And he'd roll his eyes but be all ears.

What's surprising is that at first not much changed once we all went on house arrest. I'd been on maternity leave with our second and last kid, Robyn, until the first week in March. I returned to work (another passionate subject we hashed and rehashed in Whats-App) on a Monday, settling into the butt dent of my office chair with ease and immediately sending a Slack message to the Postie Moms channel for the code to the pumping room. Two days later my boss made the announcement that we were all headed back home. Just for a few weeks. Just until the country got a handle on things. "What's the big deal," I asked my longtime writing partner, Emily, in the bathroom that afternoon. "Shouldn't we just not be gross and, like, wash our hands." But secretly I was relieved. Stepping out of the revolving glass doors an hour later with rock hard boobs fit to crack open, I was thrilled. More bra-free quiet time at home? More time to sit idly on the couch scrolling through WhatsApp? Sounded like the perfect panic-room vacation to me. Then the gunshots came.

In those first few weeks home felt almost primal, finally living up to its truest definition as not just the place one lives but the place one survives. Where we could barricade ourselves against everything happening on the other side of our door. Outside bad. Inside good. Caveman shit. But the novelty wore off when we realized the invention of fire was a long way off. Two weeks turned into four and daycares weren't going to open anytime soon. Our children could not subsist on hours of YouTube yoga and FaceTime with Grandma, who insisted on shouting every syllable as if reaching through the void of the internet. The WhatsApp chat went from daily distraction to postcards from the edge. Four weeks turned to two months and nothing made sense anymore. Nowhere was safe, really. Nothing was constant. Nothing was guaranteed. Save the WhatsApp group.

Then, on a Monday evening in May, four Minneapolis police officers respond to a call about George Floyd, a forty-six-year-old father from Texas who'd lost his job at a restaurant when the pandemic hit. Floyd allegedly purchased cigarettes from a corner store with a fake twenty. After struggling to get him into a patrol car, officers yank Floyd from the backseat onto the street's pavement, where he ends up facedown with three men shoving their weight into his body. "I can't breathe, man," he pleads. "Please." One of those officers drives his knee into Floyd's neck for what the world first thinks is an excruciating eight minutes and forty-six seconds but turns out to be an even worse nine minutes and twenty-nine seconds. Floyd begs more than a dozen times for air that never comes. Less than twenty minutes later he is dead. With some of his last breaths Floyd gasps, "Mama. Mama."

Processing George Floyd's death was almost out of the question. I couldn't and neither could Rob. It was too much on top of being on top of one another. Add more to the pile and we'd cave for real. So we grieved separately and silently as the Black Lives Matter movement erupted like a righteous volcano, cheering it on from the supposed safety of our home. Because we live in Washington— America's front lawn—we expected the protests and the loud justice to drown our city. We welcomed the flood but didn't want to be there when the dam finally burst. None of us could breathe underwater. And there were the girls to consider. Oh, and the gunshots. *Pop pop pop. Pop pop pop.* As May gave way to June and the nights got as short as our collective temper, the real start of an urban summer—asking your neighbor, "Was that fireworks or . . . ?"— became much less quaint.

Claustrophobia is one thing. Feeling like a sitting duck is another. Fuck Covid. Fuck the police. Fuck everybody. We had to get out. So, in the bougiest escape plan ever, we drove to the Myrtle Beach condo that Rob's godmother has owned since the 1980s (yes, they were among the first Black families to buy in the building, and yes, as soon as we pulled up we immediately hopped on Zillow, and yes, our "second house before the first house" dreams were quickly crushed). Despite our unofficial ban on the news, as soon as the

four of us stepped through the door I turned the TV to a local station to check the weather. A lady was in front of a map that looked
like it'd been used to clean a ketchup spill. Covid cases were spik-
ing. The whole county was red with them. "Great," I said, just as
Sally asked for the fifty-eleventh time when we were going to beach.
Yeah, we got Covid.

Honestly, there was no way around it. It was the South (sorry,
not sorry) and zero people were wearing masks or social distancing
or even thinking. The first time I walked to the pool, with Sally
holding my hand and Robyn strapped to my chest, a white-haired
man in an unbuttoned Tommy Bahama shirt reached out and
stroked my baby's arm with his finger. "Cute little thing," he said by
way of praise. Can a face look murder-y? I hoped mine did. But he
just smiled and headed to the lobby to spread more unsolicited
cheer and coronavirus. Also, did I mention that my husband never
met a stranger and likes to talk with his mouth open? Exactly. By
the time we got back to D.C. and realized we were sick I was ready
for a divorce. But then who would take care of the kids after I died
alone in an uncontrollable coughing fit on a living room floor
strewn with toys my ungrateful children refused to pick up? I was
stuck.

To add insult to infection, when Covid came crashing into our
lives my body was already worn out. I'd been working like a woman
possessed since Sally was born—or perhaps like a woman without
rich parents who provided down payments. I took a "break" during
my second maternity leave to write a book about Congresswoman
Maxine Waters. At one of my first postpartum visits I'd been handed
a sheet of paper while dressed in the same. On it was a list of stupid
questions meant to assess my mental health, gauging the temperature between one and five of just how anxious, overwhelmed, or
whatever I was. I made the mistake of answering honestly. When
Dr. Jackson came in to see me twenty minutes later, she dramati-

cally pulled said sheet from her stack of papers and said, "According to this you might be having a breakdown?" I shrugged it off. Who wasn't?

Motherhood was catching up with me. Motherhood was beating the shit out of me. I wanted to tell her to back up. I wanted to tell her to calm down. I wanted someone to find us in a dark alley going at it and yell, "Stop! Stop! Leave her alone. She's had enough." But there was no tap-out. I had to find a way to handle the ring like a pro, because we were only in round one. And did I mention the cancer scare that came before the breakdown diagnosis and the Covid infection?

"Your thyroid is enlarged," announced my new primary care doctor during a routine physical that I had scheduled only because I wanted a day off.

"I have cancer?!" See how calm I was being?

"Um, let's get you checked out," said Dr. Medley, a Black woman with salt-and-pepper hair like sheep's wool and a penchant for floral print that made me think she didn't have time to shop, which was comforting. The woman was busy saving lives!

I had an ultrasound scheduled for the next day and therefore twenty-four hours to get my affairs in order before I died. The step-down diagnosis was hypothyroidism, which after reading the symptom list seemed a lot like a disease called motherhood: exhaustion, dry skin, weight gain, lethargy, brain fog, hair loss, difficulty falling asleep, dry mouth, super PMS, and mood swings toward the dark side. I called my husband.

"You're killing me, Smalls," I told Rob. "Like for real for real." It turns out I did not have cancer, just life. I'd spent the past few years trying to be superhuman without the cool origin story, and my regular ole human body couldn't take the abuse. So Covid? It was kind of a relief.

The first people I told were the Super Cool Moms, because I

knew they wouldn't judge me. They wouldn't interrogate me. They'd say the thing they wished someone would say to them, because in that group we led with our motherness. I was on the couch, coughing and scrolling, scrolling and coughing. We'd been having a not-so-random conversation about race, which was becoming increasingly common in the wake of the reckoning. Tina had sent her Trump-loving in-laws a video of HGTV stars Chip and Joanna Gaines talking to their rack of kids about race—because if not them, then who? "Yeah, this was . . . interesting," I wrote back after watching the clip. Tina herself was clearly secondhand embarrassed by the video, but she said her conservative Christian in-laws, who loved shouting about God but found talk about racism impolite, were into it. I got it. Something was better than nothing. Then another coughing fit hit me, and I figured it was time to let the cat out of the bag.

"Also, on a completely unrelated note. No one go to Myrtle Beach. Ever," I pivoted, explaining to the group that we'd gotten "the 'rona" and that, yes, "It was horrible."

And like I thought, the Super Cool Moms immediately went into mom mode. Not friend mode or *my* mom's mode (which included lots of platitudes but no actual help), but just good old-fashioned "Let's take care of you" mode. Meghan was incensed that no one in South Carolina was taking the virus seriously. She had stats on it. Carly immediately got on the phone with her older sister, who was a doctor, and forwarded me all her recommendations in a bullet-pointed email. Mira had heard of an experimental new treatment and maybe had a connect. She was working the lines. They all just got it. Instead of piling on completely appropriate questions like "What the fuck were you guys thinking?" they sent us two hundred dollars on GrubHub. They asked if they could drop off more food, run to the pharmacy, donate breast milk if mine was waning. I mean, that last one I made up, obviously, but these were the kind of women who'd do it, no doubt. I was at the end of my rope and the WhatsApp moms gave me some slack.

Previously, I'd wasted too much time wondering not only if I fit in but if fitting in was even the goal. But none of the Super Cool Moms gave a damn about any of that. They just wanted to help. That's when I realized that over the years these women, most of whom I rarely saw IRL once Covid became our reality, were in fact some of my closest friends, my biggest cheerleaders, and my unpaid therapists.

Scrolling through WhatsApp was like flipping through the pages of one of those cheesy one-line-a-day mom diaries. I spilled my guts about work, about being impatient with Sally, annoyed with my husband, and sick of my crying baby. I talked about my anxiety, frustrations, and triumphs without fear or filter, because in the beginning they weren't quite real, just a nebulous iCloud of moms to bitch to. But they'd become more than that as I became more of me, quietly shedding the fear of becoming someone other than the woman my twenty- and thirty-year-old selves demanded I be.

I keep thinking of the word *outlet* and what it means for the kind of professional women with pent-up everything that populated my neighborhood, my news feed. The definitions are weirdly spotty and spot on. An outlet is a release, an exit, an escape. They are also the holes in the wall we jam our electrical cords into, shooting us up with energy. Outlets sell us a bunch of discount crap we don't need. An outlet is a place where we can express ourselves, announce our thoughts. The Super Cool Moms group was all of these things. Appealing to every need at once, online, in person, and in the palm of our hands. I would never just pull the plug. It was life support.

To this day I carry with me four words Mira said during that time. For the most part our family got off unscathed. Rob just felt super tired at first, and then a few days later I got a scratch at the back of my throat, and two days after that Robyn woke up with gunk all over her nose as if she'd smashed her face into a cake made of snot. But Sally remained delightfully and nerve-rackingly three. After a week Rob and Robyn bounced back like champs, whereas I was regularly plagued with coughs that wouldn't quit and left gasping for breath and clawing at my throat. It was bad, guys.

During the third or fourth such "attack" I thought calmly, *This is it,* as I crawled my way to the kitchen from the living room to get a glass of water that my brain told me would make it all better. This was where and when I ended and left my little family to their own devices, hoping I'd instilled a love of lotion at least. It'd been a great job while I had it—mother. I made it as far as the refrigerator door when Rob came up from the basement to find me hacking up useless air on the linoleum. We called my doctor again. The one who had previously prescribed the parents of a wobbly walking baby and a threenager "rest." She told us to get to the ER immediately, but we knew that could be a death sentence, so instead we went to a private urgent care. Turns out I had pneumonia on top of Covid (and motherhood)—oh, and also some recurring asthma thing from when I was kid (who knew?). The antibiotics and inhaler were a godsend. I was breathing again and slightly less prone to flights of morbidity. Slightly. After I spent ten minutes typing all that out for the WhatsApp group, Mira responded thusly: "You didn't deserve this."

Corrine packs away her ukulele; class is over. The kids are cranky and phones are buzzing with reminders of Zooms that should've been emails. In short, it's time to slink back to our respective hothouses of Magna-Tiles and *Mickey Mouse Clubhouse.* But no one wants to—obviously. Not yet. So we're doing that awkward "pretending to go but really wanna stay" dance. There are six of us; we're trying to keep our toddlers from licking each other, but we're also throwing additions to the conversation over a shoulder: "Yep, Yu Ying is going hybrid" and "These were on sale!" and "She's not walking yet." Nothing earth-shattering but somehow crucial, even life-affirming, as the kids like to say.

Once the first and second waves died down, the Super Cool Moms were dying to see each other. We hired a music teacher to meet us at Crispus Attucks Park once a week at 9 A.M. to sing to our toddlers. It was ridiculous, obviously. But it was also so necessary. We even had a Halloween-themed class where all the kids dressed up and spent the next hour tugging at tutus and, in Robyn's case, antennas.

"Full on. Suburban. White lady," jokes Rob as I hustle Robyn out the door to another class with her "friends," okay, mine. I was this. This was a part of who I was. Momming with the rest of them. Yes, fine, I was the only Black girl in the bunch. Me, a card-carrying "strong Black woman" (apologies) in the overlapping ages of Donald Trump, racial reckonings (apologies again), and biblical plagues. With all those circles tightening around me, why on earth would I volunteer to wrap myself up in a group of mothers made up almost entirely of women I used to roll my eyes at—white women in the era of Karen? But I did. And weren't they different from those hysterical ladies who lived on our phones? At least to me they were. But perhaps that wasn't enough. Or perhaps it was.

The night Kamala Harris (oh, and Joe Biden) won the presidential election, WhatsApp was abuzz with girl power and whatnot. But I wanted to point out the Blackness of it all, making sure to claim Kamala for myself. She was more mine, right? Black, in a sorority, went to undergrad at the school down the street from me. Yes and no. Angie and Priya had their hands raised too. A mixed-race Indian American woman their kids could look up to. A high-achieving South Asian daughter of an exacting mom. Nancy pointed out that Kamala was the daughter of immigrants. So she was hers too. Well after the kids had gone to bed, we were still typing back and forth about colorism, the one-drop rule, being a double minority, social hierarchies, and cultural taboos. Priya lamented the fact that her daughter had gone to sleep too early to get a picture in front of the TV with Kamala. However, Priya wasn't coming down from cloud nine, because "*I'm the daughter!!!* As are all of us," she added. But I felt that first part in my chest. I'm the daughter. We're all the daughters.

See, I really did like these women. And yet I always felt the need to mentally defend that fact to myself, because the truth was nobody else really cared. I mean, my other friends clowned me for my mom-group evangelism, but the anxiety was all my own. Really it was about *authenticity*, a frustrating word that has the power to define while also skirting definition. What did it mean? Who was my authentic self? Why place so much mental stock in some chick I didn't even know like that? A version of me that wasn't fully realized yet. Because if hiding behind every potential interaction, relationship, or group is some feared "fakeness" no one can pinpoint, then we're all just running scared from the very thing that might help us understand ourselves. Right? At least that's what I kept telling myself when I was caught laughing hysterically, nodding silently in agreement, or parroting some nugget from the Super Cool Moms.

How do we define our own me-ness? Is it always drawn outside the lines of others? Measuring myself up against all the alleged "good mom tropes" strolling through the neighborhood obviously wasn't working. It had stressed me out so much that my thyroid, an organ (?) I previously wasn't sure I even had, was basically telling me, "Bitch, you need to pump the brakes." Add to that mental breakdowns, Covid, pneumonia. Girl, if anyone needed an Rx for a chill pill, it was me. Instead of running myself ragged about what kind of mother I was, why not just admit there was no blueprint? I was becoming whatever mother, whatever person, I was supposed to be. Your authentic self doesn't arrive via stork, you have to search it out yourself.

Once, the godmother of *Becoming* and mom-in-chiefing, *the* Michelle Obama, personally gave me some advice that I promptly ignored.

This was right before Rob and I got married. I was covering a fancy-pants event at a super swank house in Washington. My plan was to get in, take some notes, and then get out with enough time to watch an *Angel* rerun. When I got wanded by Secret Service in the garage I figured maybe Valerie Jarrett was there, or even Second Lady Jill Biden, whom I'd met before. That is not a humblebrag, promise. Once I got inside and had a glass of champagne, the gorgeous and tall Black woman with the perfect bounce to her hair didn't immediately register as the woman whose entire existence served as my vision board. I just thought, *I have to ask that lady where she got that haircut. And that dress. And that nail color. And that general aura of amazingness.*

"Can you believe she came," whispered my friend Aba, who sidled up to me with her iPhone already in camera mode.

"Who?" I was still feverishly taking notes in my own phone and barely looking up.

"The first lady, girl!"

I played it cool for the next hour and a half, because who wants to be the yokel who gets gunned down while attempting to hug Michelle Obama. The plan was to look normal by taking more notes, while secretly recording everything Mrs. Obama did. 8:20: FLOTUS laughs like a human being. 8:22: FLOTUS's arms are not a myth. 8:27: FLOTUS continues to walk on earth and has yet to ascend to the heavens. And so on.

It was Aba who made me actually talk to her. I was trying to blend in near a sofa, ready to sneak a picture for her, when I looked up and was suddenly being introduced.

". . . and this is Helena Andrews," Aba said, graciously pulling me into the conversation.

"You look familiar," said the First Freaking Lady of these United States to yours truly. "I think we've met before."

After recovering from a mild seizure, I managed to say something like, "Ah, no, um, I don't think so. I write for *The Post* so maybe . . ."

She looked suspicious when I mentioned I was a reporter (damn it!), but her smile came back almost immediately. She then rubbed my arm, which I immediately vowed to smell later. The only thing I could think to ask her about was my impending marriage. I figured whatever advice she gave me would last a lifetime; plus if anything went wrong, I could always say, "Well, Michelle Obama made me do it" and all would be forgiven.

"Hmmm, that's a longer conversation over cocktails," said Mrs. Obama (if she had invited me to cosmos on my actual wedding day, I would have canceled the whole damn thing). "But most important, make sure you're always your authentic self. If you try too hard to be someone you're not, it won't work. That's what's sustained Barack and I for all these years."

I nodded like an idiot and listened more as she told me not to "trip on the wedding" even if one of my girlfriends showed up in the wrong thing. "It's just one day."

What stuck was her commandment to be my authentic self. This was a direct command from the forever first lady. To ignore it would be treason. But just who the heck was she, my authentic self, that is? I noodled the question for years after that night. In the years since, I'd become a wife and a mother. I was a daughter and friend. Did I know exactly what those versions of me looked like or had the mugshots changed over time? Perhaps all the exhaustive work I was doing to raise perfect children and be the perfect mother was just another way to hide that authentic self, to bury her under expectations that didn't matter to anyone, not even me when I really thought about it. If that was the case then the Mamas, the Super Cool Moms, all of them, weren't women to necessarily emulate or even be embarrassed by. We held up mirrors to each other even if the reflections weren't always the same.

Maya Angelou once said, "We have to confront ourselves." Me, myself, and I were due for a face-to-face-to-face. What I realized eventually is that the fantasy that fueled my twenties? I'd needed that. We all do. I needed to feel like the invincible heroine in a silk headscarf fighting off evil questions about why I hadn't found a man. As the years stacked up, I had dreamt up another fantasy to pull me through the next decade. This one filled with babies and momming so hard. And now that picture needed some serious retouching, somehow reconciling it with the old ones. To really confront who I was as a mother, a Black mother, I'd have to give birth yet again. The emotional labor pains were the worst but my authentic self was in there somewhere.

CHAPTER 5

Ain't I a Gentrifier?

"I'm really invested in you guys getting that house," said Carly when I told her that our landlords were finally warming to the idea of us buying the row house we'd moved into shortly before Sally was born. She and her husband had just bought a place two blocks away after renting for years. The global pandemic set off a buying boom in the group—moms wanted more space, more support, more safety. Leah sold her condo on North Capitol in less than a week and was moving to Vermont, naturally. Tiffany and her brood decided to decamp to "the other side of Rock Creek," which was code for where the really rich white people go. She was almost shy about it, having been raised in what I imagined was a shack (isn't that how everyone in Appalachia lived?) but turned out to be a modest rancher. Zillow and Redfin were like religions, links to dream homes passed around like relics. All the Mamas were mini real estate evangelists, and I, naturally, got swept up in the fervor.

Can a place be a personality trait? In more cinematic settings, the neighborhood plus mom equation was firmly proven. There are the nice white moms of Brooklyn, the borderline insane mothers of the Upper East Side, the orange mommies in Orange County, and on and on the stereotypes flow. Does the neighborhood define you or the other way around? In Bloomingdale, a collection of blocks that had cycled through so many different versions, Kanye West–style, it was hard to tell where one identity began and another ended. Actually, it wasn't that hard at all. Just follow the notes of bachata, salsa, and mariachi blaring from the open doors of houses getting their facelifts.

Bloomingdale was a neighborhood that could claim urban cool without the traffic noise, a suburban-ish community without the guilt of moving out to Bowie. Or, if you're white, Chevy Chase. On the precipice of old and new, rich and poor, and Black and white, Bloomingdale was still figuring its shit out. Like a recent college grad backpacking through Europe before returning to the States and taking that internship their dad had lined up, the neighborhood wanted it both ways. The homegrown charm of Chocolate City with none of the calories.

Rob and I had fallen into the same trap. When I got pregnant with Sally, we were renting a "two bedroom" (read: one bedroom with a broom closet) in the old Gage School, an imposing red-brick building with Doric columns and limestone. The Craigslist ad listed its history as one of the city's exemplary elementary schools from the first half of the twentieth century like an amenity. Guys, it was listed on the National Register of Historic Places. We were sold on the big windows and the whiff of historic significance, never thinking twice about the fact that the school had remained stubbornly all white until the 1950s, even after Black neighbors, who would eventually make up the majority of the neighborhood and were jammed into overcrowded schools nearby, lobbied to be let in. We were in G107, one of the original classrooms nearest the boys' entrance, and never the wiser.

Loving the neighborhood was about seeing and not seeing. Each morning, as I walked Miles, our pug, down Second Street, I waved to the Black women in slacks and knit tops sweeping the strip of sidewalk in front of their houses. They were always glad to see *me*, as if I, a young, Black, professional woman with a ring on her finger, were the unicorn and not they, women holding on to their family homes despite the mailbox overflowing with "We Want to BUY Your House" postcards that bordered on threatening.

There were Miss Joyce, Miss Connie, and Miss Irene. And there was Mr. Fred—who everyone called Samurai—a retired French-embassy security guard who drove a red Corvette and spent most afternoons on his porch in green fatigues reading poetry. This was community. These were the characters I envisioned starring in our Netflix family sitcom. And yet I knew the only way to make that dream a reality was if one of them either died or defaulted, leaving their well-loved 1,900-square-foot home in probate court until I could swoop in with a down payment that currently existed only on my Google spreadsheet. How could I be both Valkyrie and vulture, fiercely protective of the peace these folks had carved out for themselves while secretly salivating over the possibilities?

That's what I was thinking about—death and taxes—when I spotted it: our "dream" home. The row house sat sad and empty at the top of the neighborhood. Miles and I had passed it unnoticed hundreds of times on our morning jaunts, but the big FOR RENT sign stabbed into the dying lawn was unmissable. *This is our chance,* I thought. The plan was to rent it for as long as it took to convince our landlords to sell to us, since we so obviously deserved it. That is not how home buying works. Not for us anyway. Soon we'd learn that these streets we felt so eerily connected to might have been calling us all along.

———

"So, do you guys work at Howard?" [Insert eye roll, blank stare, and teeth suck here.]

Hmmm, how to take this? On the one hand, we *are* standing on the crumbling porch of a century-old row house, which is located a light jog away from The Mecca, aka Howard University, the historically Black institution founded shortly after the Civil War. It's close. It's Black. We Black. Ipso facto presto chango, we go together. The leap isn't exactly treacherous; in fact, it's understandable.

But, ma'am.

It's a white lady asking. So start there and immediately bypass "idle chitchat." I know what this chick is trying to do. She's sorting, in the midst of determining the appropriate Black People Category to file us under. Educated? Section 8? She needs to know what *kind* of Black we are. She wants the "why." Why else would they be here? Why else would they be so well-spoken? Why else would they look so fresh? So clean? Why else?

I answer "No" without blinking or further explanation. She waits for the rest of that sentence, but it's complete. She's uncomfortable. I can tell because she laughs as if someone said something funny. I sure didn't. There's a pause, a sag in the air between us that threatens to drown the whole thing like a flash flood. Rob claps his hands together, thunder-snapping everyone back to the present.

"Should we get started?" he booms, looking pointedly at me as if to say, *Calm your hot ass down, Harriet Tubman.*

I stick my chin in the air, grab the tarnished front doorknob, and give it a twist. "Yep, let's," I say while pushing the door open, welcoming the appraiser into the house we've been renting since right before our older daughter was born. The house we're now hoping to buy from our landlords—rich developers from Virginia who are so busy with suburban pandemic renovations that they don't have time to flip our place into tight million-dollar condos. The house that three generations ago we could've been kicked out of because of "race covenants" written into the deed that prevented Black folks from renting or purchasing homes on this block. The house that was once home to a group of Howard students who hosted frat parties so epic our neighbors wept with joy when we moved in. The house with drafty windows, mice that rolled their eyes at traps, and a basement bathroom I once described as "gas station chic." The house we want so badly we drift off to sleep counting renovation projects. The house we brought both our babies home to, the house that reminds me of a TGIF sitcom set, the house I've grown in. The house we're hoping against hope this appraiser lady doesn't price us out of. Damn it, I should've told her we worked at Howard. That we were Blackety Black Black. Perhaps that would've knocked a few thousand off the sticker price.

All this is swimming in my head as the three of us step into our foyer—a fancy word for the landing strip between the front door, the ancient radiator, and the barf-color carpeted stairs. "Where," I ask, "do you want to start?"

Let's begin in Bloomingdale, a bucolic ribbon (two blocks by thirteen) of row houses developed in the late 1800s—just outside of what was then D.C. proper—that is now gentrification ground zero.

When I first arrived in 2008, I thought I'd moved on up—both literally and figuratively. Prior to that I was living in a basement apartment packed with more rats than plastic delivery forks. Then, with a new book deal and Barack Obama's bid for the White House coursing through my veins, I hightailed it to a renovated Bloomingdale one bedroom across from a trap house disguised as a trap house. Why hide it? The neighborhood knew what was up. That same summer I attempted to sublet the place because the rent was too damn high. The hardwood floors, sixteen-foot ceilings, and granite countertops were like catnip to young professionals hot off the campaign trail. Minutes after I hit "publish," my inbox swelled with a tide of scheduled "come sees." Then they actually came and saw. The cognitive dissonance was like a cold shower.

Here's a sampling of the well-mannered reactions I received once these potential subletters realized a) that the woman in possession of the professional phone voice and email platitudes was Black and b) that the neighborhood where this gorgeous apartment was situated was, if not all the way Black, then at least Black-ish, Black adjacent, Black unloading.

"Oh my God, I didn't know all this was here," as they cautiously ventured out of their cars. "What did you say this neighborhood was called again?" as they looked over their shoulders on their way up the front steps, clocking the group of boys-cum-men congregating on the stoop across the street. "It's kinda, like, hidden, huh?" as they slyly tinkered with their phones, no doubt panic-texting friends just in case they ended up missing. Then they huffed up to the fourth floor, and I opened the door to a whole new world, Aladdin-style, revealing a renter's dream.

Everyone loved the place. Nobody loved the block, which was hot before that was cool. They hid their unease expertly—smiling at the wood floors, caressing the stone countertops, oohing in the walk-in closet, and then never calling back. It was arsenic-in-your-celery-juice racism—tasteless.

But there was one unforgettable interaction that instantly went on my White People permanent record. She was a sweet, tiny Southern girl (actually, I'm assuming, because she refused to get out of her car) who wasn't just ignorantly nervous about being in proximity to the Blacks. She was terrified. I could hear it in her voice.

"Hi!" I answered in my nonthreatening phone voice. "Are you downstairs? I'll buzz you up!"

"Yeah, hi. No. I mean, yes," she replied, sounding completely discombobulated, but, like I said, the accent was Southern so maybe *I* was the asshole. *Southern people talk slow. It's fine. She'll get to the point eventually.* "Yes, I'm outside, but," she continued. "I just . . . this place. Online the apartment looked . . . lovely. But this street. Um, it's just not what I was looking for. The neighborhood, I mean. It's just . . . not what I was picturing. Is it safe? I'm sorry. I'm sorry. It's . . . I'm not going to come up."

Honestly, it took me a minute to understand what was going on. The neighborhood? Not what she had pictured? There are trees everywhere. Families. Dogs. Sure, there's a trap house on the other side of the crosswalk, but the guys are sweet. I looked out my window and waved at the crew on the stoop. They waved back with hands pierced with blunts. *Ohhhhhhhhh.* The *neeeeeighborhood.* She was scared of them, me, us.

"Okay, thanks, bye," I said, hitting the "end call" button and laughing to keep from screaming.

Eventually I sublet the place sight unseen to two Capitol Hill interns arriving from Ohio. Their only complaint was that the AC conked out twice. I never saw them, just like I never saw Tiny Southern Racist Lady, but they sounded white over the phone (just like I do most of the time). I never forgot that girl, though. I think about her when I pass that old building on the way to get my girls from daycare. It's condos now, and the former trap house across the street sold for $1.1 million last year. I wouldn't be shocked if in the years since we first "met," Tiny Southern Racist Lady had married a Democratic comms director and moved into one of the Victorians on First Street. Her kids probably play at the same park mine do. That's how quickly things changed in Bloomingdale. Or maybe the neighborhood simply went back to its roots in the same way vines bring down skyscrapers after the apocalypse. Because way back in the day this place was all white.

In a 2018 study, the internet listing service RentCafé analyzed eleven thousand U.S. zip codes to pinpoint the "most gentrified" areas in the country. *Gentrification,* for anyone living under a rock (or in a rent-stabilized apartment), is defined by Merriam-Webster as "a process in which a poor area (as of a city) experiences an influx of middle-class or wealthy people who renovate and rebuild homes and businesses and which often results in an increase in property values and the displacement of earlier, usually poorer residents."

Culling through U.S. Census Bureau data from 2001 to 2016, RentCafé measured changes in median household price, income, and education level. Guess which zip won second place in the real estate Hunger Games? Ours, 20001, a rectangular slice of the nation's capital occupying just over two square miles. In just sixteen years, home values in the 20001 zip code shot up by more than 207 percent, income by more than 163 percent, and education levels (folks with bachelor's degrees or higher) by 212 percent, according to the RentCafé analysis of what the firm called "extreme gentrifi-cation." A 2020 *Washington Post* article gave it the kiss of death, calling Bloomingdale "one of D.C.'s most-coveted addresses."

But that only tells part of the story. Gentrification is one thing, barreling through the neighborhood like a picky tornado—devouring some houses whole while leaving others completely untouched—but the lightening of Bloomingdale goes deeper. Over the decades owners have flipped from white to Black to white like bathroom tiles. It's the history of this place that's really getting gutted. These sidewalks tell a story that most of the newbies push-ing Uppababy strollers over them don't care to address. And I'm counting us among the newbies. Being Black doesn't exempt you from being a gentrifier. Sure, Miss Connie and Miss Irene—Black women who've been here since the 1970s—offer us waves from their porch quicker than they'd do for the white girls in the group house next door, but really, are we any better? Because when Miss Connie toyed with the idea of selling her house a few years ago, we made sure to stop by—with the cute babies in tow. Because I've noticed Miss Irene's grandkids don't stop by enough and maybe that big ole house is too much for her. Because it wasn't until we had lived in our house for nearly four years that we learned the area's not-so-hidden secret: that four of the six families who helped end the practice of racial covenants in America lived right here too. We'd been walking on hallowed ground for years and didn't know it.

Once home to expansive estates, orchards, and farmland owned by a handful of powerful, rich white Washingtonians, the neighborhood began to take shape in the late Victorian era. The first row houses—ornate classic brick affairs (think the opening credits of *House of Cards*)—were built by George N. Beale, whose mom and dad had owned the fifty-acre Bloomingdale Estate on which fifteen men, women, and children were enslaved. After their parents' deaths the Beale descendants subdivided the land for development. The goal was to attract middle-class (read: "white") folks to what was then considered a suburb that connected to the good government jobs downtown via a new streetcar line.

It was idyllic. There was fresh air; the houses were modern; the streets were paved. And all this came at a time when the country, and Washington especially, was experiencing a housing shortage alongside an economic boom in the long decades following the Civil War. The nation's capital and the government were expanding like a balloon. People were pouring into the city in search of newly established well-paying jobs, and they needed someplace to live. Black folks rode that wave too, fleeing the segregated South and heading to cities in the north and out west during the Great Migration. Basically, D.C was hot, and Bloomingdale was hotter.

One of the neighborhood's first Black homeowners arrived in 1907 at 2206 First Street, which was considered a premier block, with its grand, three-story homes. Francis de Sales Smith was a civil engineer and one of the first Black students to graduate from Catholic University in Washington, according to my extensive Google sleuthing. But white folks here didn't give a shit about that. Credentials would never ever outweigh color.

The good neighbors of Bloomingdale wasted no time in banding together to cancel the sale. One of those concerned citizens was Samuel Gompers, a progressive advocate for workers' rights and founder of the American Federation of Labor. He lived a block south from Mr. Smith at 2122 First Street and gave his hard-earned money to the legal fund created to get Mr. Smith gone. The allegedly nonracist logic—which was codified by federal loan policies and backed by real estate agents—was that Black homeowners inevitably brought down property values. So a majority of the quintessentially Washington row homes built in Bloomingdale had racism baked into the bricks: legally binding covenants written into property deeds that banned the sale of homes in designated "white areas" to anyone, um, not white. The deed would include language like this: "Said lot shall never be rented, leased, sold, transferred or conveyed to any Negro or colored person." Breaking this contract came with a hefty financial penalty, sometimes equal to 40 percent of the home's purchase price. The house at 2206 First Street was bound by one such covenant, and in one of the first cases brought before the local court in D.C., Mr. Smith's white next-door neighbor sued to have the sale canceled. By 1910 Mr. Smith was gone.

That was the first case. The last would come nearly forty years later, a seminal moment that would eventually abolish racially restrictive housing covenants in the whole damn country (racism, of course, was still a thing). In the decades between, the once vanilla Bloomingdale had become increasingly chocolaty. By 1920, LeDroit Park, the formerly gated all-white enclave shouldering Bloomingdale, was all Black. But Bloomingdale, which had entire blocks filled with Black homeowners and renters, still clung to its rapidly fading identity as a white neighborhood.

In 1923, nearly five hundred white homeowners in this sliver of D.C. mobilized at the corner of First and U streets with plans to march to the front doors of three Black families who lived in properties not bound by racial covenants and politely ask them to get the fuck out. There were no crosses burned, no windows shattered by bricks, no disgusting slurs scrawled in white paint on the sidewalk. But so what? Imagine it. You're about to sit down to dinner when your doorbell rings and *boom* a swarm of scowling faces greets you with a note? Instead of "threats" this allegedly civilized mob of concerned citizens hand-delivered an "ultimatum" to a Howard University professor and a Pullman porter (at the last house a woman answered the door and then, seeing the mob and a reporter's camera flash, quickly shut it again).

Here's what the note said: "These men and women here are property holders of Bloomingdale and they want you to know they resent to the limit your purchase of the property in this section and particularly your moving into the property. You may not have known that you were buying property in a white neighborhood, but whether or not you knew this, you did buy, and we want you to know that we expect you to vacate these premises. We will help you to find a purchaser for the property and will cooperate with you in any and every way possible if you will do the wise and courageous thing—move out. We know the leaders of your own race agree with this position."

According to an article in *The Evening Star*, the mob (I can't call it anything else) carried out its thuggery "peaceably." The Black homeowners read the note and provided "no comment."

The Grand Poobah of this whole affair was a Bloomingdale resident and lawyer named Henry Gilligan, who had been collecting signatures and gathering troops for the march for months. But it wasn't like he hated Black people or anything. In fact, Gilligan told *The Evening Star* that "the property holders of Bloomingdale are

not unfriendly to the colored people." They were simply determined to "save Bloomingdale for the white people." Two of the
three families refused to leave. After that there was a committee
formed to keep track of all the houses that might fall into Black
hands. Its job was to go around and secure pledges from white
homeowners that they wouldn't sell or rent to anyone not white. At
its first get-together, which was described as "packed to overflowing," the committee collected a thousand dollars to keep the neighborhood "a strictly white residential section." This was peak Secret
White Meeting. Peak.

Why, then, did Black families stay? Why did they fight? Why
move there in the first place? Why not go somewhere, anywhere
else?

Because there was quite literally nowhere else to go.

Mara Cherkasky, co-creator of the digital history project Map-
ping Segregation in Washington, D.C., put it plainly. "The houses
weren't just a little bit better, they were *a lot* better. The neighborhoods that were not restricted were the oldest and the housing was
deteriorated *and* crowded. Where were Black people allowed to
live? Where white people didn't want to—far away, in areas that
didn't have paved streets or streetlights or even sewer systems."
Every Black family moving into a house restricted by a race covenant wasn't trying to buck the system, make history, or give a middle finger to their neighbors; they were just trying to live. But if the
twenty-first century has taught us anything, Black folks just trying
to live continues to be a sticking point for some white people.

I can't imagine trying to raise a family amid all that open hostil-
ity and fragility. But, then again, of course I can. The history of
Bloomingdale is barely history at all. It's as if time has folded in on
itself and here I am, Blackety Black and proud, playing the baby
bongos with women whose faces could have been those in that

U Street mob. Women who, as we stroll side by side down First Street together after meeting for mommy happy hour, go about their lives unbothered by ghosts.

Which brings us to Lena Hodge.

On a fall evening in 1909, Lena, twenty-seven, married Frederic Hodge, thirty-two, in a ceremony held at her parents' home in leafy Capitol Hill, according to the wedding announcement in *The Washington Times*. After a month-long "northern bridal tour," the newlyweds settled at 136 Bryant Street NW, then a brand-spanking-new two-story row home built on the northern edge of Blooming-dale and purchased for seven thousand dollars. One of the reasons the couple was drawn to the neighborhood was its status as an all-white enclave. The racial covenant in their deed was a selling point.

In census records, Lena, who had some education but didn't go to college, is usually listed as a homemaker—though in 1930 she briefly declared herself an "artist." Her father was a music teacher, and she sang. Fred had a good gig as the chief of supplies for the U.S. Department of Agriculture. The couple never had children and lived in the house on Bryant into their old age. An active member in the Order of the Eastern Star and the neighborhood's citizens' association, Lena would later be described as "the big chief" of the block by the Black families she made it her personal mission to kick out.

Lena and I would've been neighbors, but obviously never friends. Walking up and down her street now, I wonder what Lena would have thought of me. Of the thirty addresses that made up her block, eleven had strict racial covenants and the rest did not. Over the years Black families began moving into houses on the western end of the street. Lena wasn't blind. She would have seen Black people coming in from work, tending their front yards, having a cool drink on their porches. Would she have waved? Spat? Shook her damn head? Perhaps all three, depending on her mood. Who knows? What we do know is that the idea of living shoulder to shoulder with Black folks was too much for Lena, the big chief.

In 1947, she sued a Black family who'd moved into one of the three-story Victorian-style homes at the eastern end of the block. That case would eventually make its way to the Supreme Court as part of a landmark decision that abolished the legal enforcement of racial covenants across the country. Lena had no way of knowing her fight would be the starting round of the modern-day Civil Rights Movement. She just wanted the Black people on her block to go away. Never mind that by this point Bloomingdale as a whole was more than 40 percent Black. Despite a flimsy racial dividing line on First Street with an ever-shortening chain of white-occupied row homes, the neighborhood was very clearly changing. But Lena would do her damnedest to hold on to her shrinking white superiority.

The first Black couple to buy a house on Bryant Street, James and Mary Hurd, purchased the stately Victorian at 116 Bryant in the spring of 1944. After World War II, the pull of federal jobs increased Washington's Black population from 187,000 to over 280,000. And Bloomingdale was a good place to set down roots— bucolic, adjacent to a historically Black college and LeDroit Park's established Black elite.

Mr. Hurd, a welder, recalled meeting Lena on move-in day. She wasted zero time, confronting Mr. Hurd while he was in the middle of carrying furniture into his newly purchased home. The two chatted briefly, during which time Lena politely informed the grown man before her that his efforts were for naught.

"It is just too bad, because this may be a case of your having to move out . . . because some other ones have moved out that have gone into these houses," she told Mr. Hurd, according to his own testimony at trial. Lena laid it on thick, having probably delivered this speech before, telling him that all the "elderly people" on the block would probably have to move "if the colored come in."

"I don't want anything to force me out of my home," she added. "That is probably what you are going to do here." Mr. Hurd did what a lot of Black folk did, and still do, when faced with the ridiculousness of racism. He tried logic, respectability. He told Lena that she and her cohort would "find out that we will be as clean as a lot of white ones will."

"That isn't the issue," she countered. The covenant had been violated. See, it was just a legal thing, a contractual thing, not like racism or whatever. Remember, it was "just too bad," according to Lena. And with that Lena Hodge left James Hurd on his stoop, followed the curved sidewalk back to her, ahem, more modest two-story row house, and called her partner-in-prejudice, Henry Gilligan. The same man who, two decades earlier, had led a white mob through the neighborhood to root out the Blackness.

Henry Gilligan and Lena Hodge cracked open their Big Book of Bigotry and got to work. First, Gilligan called Mr. Hurd to inform him once again that the deed's "All white people or else!" agreement had been violated. Thing is, Mr. Hurd knew about the covenant when he bought the house and didn't give a fig about it. He was light-skinned enough to pass for white, was listed as "mulatto" on the census, and claimed that he wasn't even Black, so bloop. His wife, Mary, was also light-skinned, an orphan who wasn't sure what her racial makeup was exactly. As far as the Hurds were concerned, that dumb-ass covenant didn't even apply to them. Okay, okay, fine, these two probably knew full well they were Black. We always know. But if the "law" itself was this absurd then why not fuck with it a little bit?

By the late fall of 1944, the Hurds still hadn't budged. Equally undeterred, Gilligan and Lena called a neighborhood meeting at the Hodge residence a few doors down. I imagine the tiny living

room and dining room—just like ours—packed elbow to elbow
with people salivating over the audacity of those Negroes up the
street and I cackle. My heart also breaks for the Hurds. By the end
of that meeting a formal complaint for court action was in motion.
But the universe had something for they racist asses.

Ten months later, Robert and Isabella Rowe moved next door to
the Hurds at 118 Bryant. Then, in rapid succession, two other
Black families purchased homes on the block. Pauline Stewart and
her kin settled into 150 Bryant. Stewart, along with four members
of her extended family, had been evicted from their previous home
(something that happened a lot and without cause to Black folks,
who already felt the housing squeeze tighter than most), and they
were in desperate need of a place to settle down. When Ms. Stewart's realtor told her about 150 Bryant, he informed her, alluding to
the race covenant, that she'd be "taking a chance." Oh, and if she
wanted it, Ms. Stewart would have to make an offer without stepping through the front door. She took it. Last came the Savages,
Herbert and Georgia, who moved to 134 Bryant, right next to
Lena. Ain't that about a bitch?

Now four Black families owned homes on Bryant Street.

Hurd v. Hodge first went to trial in 1945. The Hurds, who didn't
plan on going anywhere, turned to the NAACP for help. It dis-
patched legal legend Charles Hamilton Houston, who'd transformed
Howard University School of Law from a night program to a prestigious institution focused on racial justice. Houston was familiar
with the area, having defended other Black Bloomingdale residents
in covenant cases. He had yet to win one but was deep in the fight.
For the Hurds, Houston's courtroom plan of attack had an inven-
tive, three-pronged approach. First, he argued that the Hurds weren't
even Black so the anti-Black language in the deed didn't apply.

"What," Houston asked Lena's husband, Frederic Hodge, at
trial, "is a negro [*sic*] about Mr. Hurd's features?"

Mr. Hodge's reply? "I would say the nose for one thing . . . the nostrils, the lower part of the nose." *Mmmmkay.* So, based on the circumference of his nose and his slightly darker than see-through skin, Mr. Hurd should be summarily evicted from the home he bought with his hard-earned American money dollars?

Next, Houston moved on to Lena. Oh, Lena. The lady who once said that she'd rather live next to a white criminal than a Black doctor. How, Houston wanted to know, did Lena know she was white?

"How do you know you are a Negro?" Lena snapped. Houston clapped back, "I know that, because you all say I am." The exchange was intense, and it was also a brilliant tactic. Its sole purpose was to air out the absurdity of race as a concept.

Houston's final strategy was to argue that the neighborhood wasn't even "white," per se. How could it be, with the browning of Bloomingdale nearing 40 percent? Lastly, Houston claimed that the notion that Black people brought down property values was completely false. In fact, it was the opposite. He got white neighbors to admit in court that their Black counterparts kept up their homes and were clean and cordial. Keeping Black people out while row homes sat empty due to white flight for the exurbs was counterintuitive. If anything, race covenants were doing more harm than good when it came to property values.

Despite Houston's best efforts, he and the Hurds lost at trial and then again on local appeal. But by this time anti-covenant cases were rising across the country and the Hurds, along with the Rowes, Stewarts, and Savages, took their case to the Supreme Court. It was argued as a companion to yet another anti-covenant case out of Saint Louis, *Shelley v. Kraemer.*

The courtroom was filled to bursting on the January morning in 1948 when oral arguments for *Hurd v. Hodge* were presented before the court. The mood was thick. Spectators knew that whatever happened this would be a watershed moment. Henry Gilligan, the real estate lawyer who'd for decades made it his mission to keep Black people out of Bloomingdale—or at least make it known that they were in no way welcome—maintained that he had "no racial prejudice whatever." All of this, Gilligan reasoned before the justices, was simply a question of law and order. The covenants, as maintained by local courts throughout the country, were legal, private contracts between sellers. It wasn't about oppressing Black people, it was about personal taste, one's individual right to live among one's own.

In the highest courtroom in the land, Gilligan argued that prejudice was cool, instinctive even. "Discrimination," he told the court, "is as much a law of nature as gravity." There was "nothing disgraceful" about it, he added.

Houston didn't mince his words, going just as hard against as Gilligan did for. "Racism in the United States must stop," he said.

Four months later, the Supreme Court handed down its unanimous decision overturning the lower courts' judgment in *Hurd v. Hodge* and declared the judicial enforcement of racially restrictive deed covenants unconstitutional. There was more legalese, of course, but the long and short of it was simple. That shit had to stop. Racism in general and racism in real estate would continue, obviously. But no longer could someone like Lena Hodge and her henchman Henry Gilligan take Black neighbors to court and expect a judge to order their eviction. That was over with.

Upon hearing the decision, Pauline Stewart's eighty-three-year-old father thanked God. Another Black neighbor told a reporter that things would have to change eventually. "This is America, brother," he said.

For their part, Lena and Fred Hodge vowed to stay on Bryant. They were in their sixties and seventies by then. Where else would they go? But another white family on the block, the Purdues, originally of Georgia, were resolved in the opposite direction. They told reporters that the Black families on the block were "fine neighbors" but that their house would be up for sale posthaste. When asked why, Mrs. Purdue was succinct: "I'm white."

By 1960 more than 99 percent of Bloomingdale was Black. That's the place that Miss Connie, Miss Irene, Miss Joyce, Samurai, and their families know. The Black Bloomingdale. The Bloomingdale of porch parties and neighbors who looked like you and waved hello. The Bloomingdale of working-class normal folk. That *other* place, filled with Lena Hodges and her confederates, no longer existed to them. The very name, Bloomingdale, was practically forgotten.

From there and for a Pandora's boxful of reasons—including white flight, Black middle-class flight, and government divestment— the neighborhood began to show its slip. What had existed before— the place that fought so hard to resist change, clinging to the past like oxygen—had been ripped up from its roots, leaving scored ground in its wake. Lower-income Black households were left to do the tending—building community centers out of abandoned lots and roaming the neighborhood in orange hats to scare off drug dealers. Then, after more decades, another economic upswing, the city's urban DC Cool (that was the actual name of a local tourism campaign) revival, and Barack Obama's arrival, Bloomingdale gets a shout-out in the *Washington Post* real estate section. It's as if it awakened magically from a medically induced coma, then promptly forgot the caregivers who'd been wiping its ass without thanks for all those years.

Admittedly we knew little about the history of Bloomingdale when we moved into our row house not far from Lena's own. We knew nothing about the ghosts of giants hovering over our splintered porch and the cracked sidewalk. The forgotten memories of families who looked like us and wanted to live someplace clean, safe, and quiet. What we did know was that our house was below market and unloved, and we hoped to own it one day. But in case that didn't work out, like carpetbagging gentrifiers, we eyed the decaying homes of our older Black neighbors while they complained to us about "all these white people" moving onto the block. Were we white people in sheep's clothing? I mean, no, obviously. But maybe a little? The internal conflicts!

"This would be *such* a great opportunity for you guys," said the appraiser as she walked through our house and catalogued its guts, marking everything down in a notebook she cradled in her left arm like an attending physician. Once again, I wondered what she meant by that. For us? Why, because we're Black! Or maybe also because the neighborhood was approaching scalding and we were poised to get a "steal." Her comment existed somewhere in that greige area.

And she was right, of course. It *would* be a great opportunity. We could reclaim a space that was never meant for us but had once been ours and was now on the verge of being snatched away in the tidal wave of gentrification. It's hard to explain how fiercely we felt the historic loss, as if we were somehow native to this place and not gentrifiers like everyone else. But once home gets into your bones it's hard to excise the feeling. And once you know home was hard-won, then it's almost impossible. Leaving would be disloyal.

And remember I had house fever, which much like baby fever is contagious. We were deep into the global pandemic and nesting took on new meaning. All the moms I knew in the neighborhood were reevaluating what home meant to them, whether it was "back home" with parents out west or a backyard in the suburbs. We were still figuring out what home meant for us, as Black parents. Did it mean history, belonging, winning? Could we abandon the dream of making the house we lived in truly ours, the same dream the Hurds had? Trailing behind the woman tasked with appraising our walls, deciding on the value of place, I still wasn't sure.

My friend the poet and professor LeConté Dill put it best in a poem she wrote called "The Fourth of You Lie," whose title I love because on hot nights in a neighborhood like ours you really do wonder if the pop you heard after midnight was from the good kind of gunpowder.

And maybe the feds did supply the hood with fireworks
And maybe the fireworks will scare the gentrifiers away
And maybe the gentrifiers will leave the hood
And maybe I'm a gentrifier
And maybe I hate to admit that
And maybe I'm not scared of fireworks
And maybe I will leave the hood for another hood
And maybe the hood be home

CHAPTER 6

The Invisible Mom

We were at the playground with Sally when it happened. The inevitable. The moment my Spidey-senses, sharpened over a lifetime of being Black on both sides, had always known was coming. White people were gonna white, and a trapdoor would swing open revealing an empty space below that was less escape hatch and more black hole. It would suck us in, erase our existence. Damn, that sounds profound, doesn't it? It was. And the entire experience was brought to us by a kid from the projects.

My mother is holding a child not her own nearly three inches off the ground by his ankles. I'm so impressed by her brute strength, especially given her bum arm, that I don't say anything helpful like "Please stop." The boy is maybe seven, maybe twelve. We don't know because we've never seen this kid before. We're at the playground, and they aren't playing.

"Why are you doing this?" he asks in a way that is more generally inquisitive than accusatory.

"Are you calm? Is the blood rushing to your head?" she answers by way of not answering. She waits, still holding him up like a fat chicken on its way to the guillotine.

"Mmmm, yes?"

"Okay then."

Frances gingerly lays him down on the rainbow-colored rubber surface. First his head, then neck, then each vertebra of his petite spine. "There now," she says. "You good?"

He nods, picks himself up off the ground, and then immediately shoots across the playground in the direction of the little white girl he'd been terrorizing before my mother got to him.

"Jesus Christ," I sigh, shaking my head from a safe distance. "Homie won't quit."

Tiffany and I had planned a late afternoon playdate at the newly built playground in our neighborhood. The place used to be an elementary school. Then the neighborhood flipped and it was just an empty eyesore, a mausoleum for a dying D.C. The neighborhood flipped again, but this time to the good side of the coin, and the whole building got razed and turned into a park complete with a gazebo, a jogging path, a field, and two dog parks. "I knew as soon as they tore it down there'd be kids back here again," an old porch lady told me once as I strolled past her house to the park. It was a chicken-and-egg-type thing. I was just glad my daughter didn't have to reach for the monkey bars at the other "playground" across the street that was nestled in front of "the condos" (our secret code word around white people for the projects). Yes, the sparkling new thanks-to-gentrification park was situated right next to the pj's.

This fact rarely bothered me. I hated when Sally was "the only one" on the swings and relished when she chased around the big kids who looked like her. So when Tiffany, who never pretended to know what she was doing and whose daughter had resting bitch face, suggested we meet up at The Park at LeDroit, I was all in. The kids screamed down the slide as we looked on, both bored and delighted. Our husbands laughed about work. My mom scrolled through her phone near the strollers. It was fine. Then we all heard it.

"Ahhhhh. No! Stop it," screeched a little white girl who looked to be about nine, tall for her age and scared for her life. She was sprinting away from a little Black boy who looked determined. I tried to ignore it. Rob, Sally, my mom, and I were the only other Black people at the playground besides this hooligan, and well, unlike Vegas, whatever happens here ends up on the listserv.

"No, no, *nooooo!*" The girl was getting louder, and the boy wasn't letting up. He'd pushed her off her bike and was now triumphantly circling the playground with a shit-eating grin. They did this cat-and-mouse thing over and over, with the violence ratcheting up a notch. That's when Frances got involved, what led her to grab the little boy midrun and turn him on his head, hoping the change in scenery might help maybe. But, of course, it didn't. This dude was no joke. I could see something brewing, something crazy happening, someone calling the police, someone dying. I elbowed Rob, hard.

"Do something," I said.

"Like what?"

"I don't know. Help."

The girl screams again as if she's been stabbed through the heart as the little boy pushes her to the ground with one hand while yanking her irresistibly shiny bike away with the other. You gotta admire little man's technique. He's a pro—rolling his eyes at her shouts, hopping on the bike, and then hitting *The Fast and the Furious*–level donuts around the jungle gym. My mom runs over to intervene once more, but Rob stops her. "Hold on, Frances," my husband says before she can once again gently manhandle this child we do not know. "I got it."

What exactly "it" means is complicated in ways only Black parents can truly recognize. The playground is not just for playing, not for us anyway. Parents of Black children are on high alert when they step through those iron gates, always looking out for the sand traps near the sandboxes. Those innocent-seeming "kids being kids" interactions that threaten to swallow their baby girls' self-confidence unless we keep up the "I hope you're being nice!" helicoptering around the blond girls they're "playing" with. In a rapidly gentrified neighborhood like Bloomingdale, where people of every color and credit score parent in proximity, the possibilities of getting "it" wrong are endless. Therefore, it's our double duty to make sure our little ones don't crack their heads open jumping off the goddamn slide and that their hearts stay whole after playing with white kids. Now, this particular baby boy causing all the ruckus isn't ours, but he is. So we're doing "it."

Begrudgingly, my husband trots over to the girl and her father, who are now both backed into a corner like potential roadkill, as they tried to fend off this little boy who really wanted that damn bike.

By the looks of him, he's from "the condos." Rob and I both grew up as the kind of poor kids who never knew they were poor but who everybody else knew were poor. Actually no, that's not right. We knew because other folks (read: horrible first graders, "well-meaning" adults, free-lunch tickets, etc.) pointed it out. But poor never meant unloved or uncared-for. We had plenty growing up. It was the overabundance of "stuff" that we lacked. This kid seems like that. Game recognizes game. Little man's clothes are simultaneously too big and too small. His fuzzy cornrows are days past their prime. His shoes are fraying knockoffs of knockoffs. And his parents are nowhere to be found. He's ripping through the playground like a pinball in a machine, catapulting from the gate and dinging against every section until it hurts. The three of us—me, my mom, and my husband—want nothing more than to wrap this ball of energy up long enough to give the rest of the kids (including our toddler) a breather. Or at least the girl with the bike time to pedal home. Homie is not here for that. He came to play, and that bike, glittery and new, never stood a chance.

"My man, my man," says Rob as he lays his baseball-mitt hands gently over the boy's, delicately loosening each of his tight little fingers off the handlebars one by one. "This is hers. You had your turn, right?"

"But I want it!" he whines, the tone giving away his age more than his previous tough-guy routine.

"Sure, sure," says Rob. "But it's *hers*." The emphasis here is for us only. It says without saying it, *You can't be harassing these little white kids like this, dude.* Problem is this little boy hasn't gotten that secret memo yet, and secretly I hope he never does.

The girl's father, a short dude with shaggy dark brown hair in a T-shirt touting a band I'd never heard of, seems to finally realize the situation isn't going to magically resolve itself. That an adult should probably step in when little ones—Black or no—are straight-up fighting each other. Actually, I'm sure Band Dad knew full well this wasn't normal behavior, but he was giving this little boy from the projects some extra runway. That's another funny thing I've noticed, and by funny, I mean highly hypocritical: Certain nice white people in our neighborhood are very cautious about correcting Black kids—in person. I've seen this happen on the playground, at the public pool, the bodega, and the farmer's market. These are the same folks who won't hesitate to describe a robbery suspect as "Black male, average build, 12–45 years old" on the Nextdoor app. But to say something IRL to a little Black boy bothering your daughter? That was apparently a hair too far. And trust Tiffany and her husband are watching this entire scene play out with a mixture of horror and relief that they don't have to get involved. We, the

Blacks, are handling our own—apparently. Sigh. Anyway, back to the bike.

Band Dad, Rob, the little boy, and the white girl are all huddled up now like a team preparing for the next big play. Would they fake right? Left? Punt? When they break, each kid happily heads to their own corner of the playground. Peace. Finally. Rob returns to tickling one-year-old Sally on the swings while singing a song they made up about feet. I join Frances on a nearby bench to quietly marvel at the scene I never starred in as a kid—a dad loving up on his daughter. The two of us watch silently satisfied. Then there's that scream again.

"Oh, for fuck's sake!" I hiss, throwing my hands up in Rob's direction. *Come on, my guy.*

Rob steps in for one last round of Save This Little White Girl, who's now biking around the playground like a hamster on a wheel trying to outpedal the little boy, whose energy knows no bounds. Once he catches her for the umpteenth time, the little boy goes from playful pushing to straight shoving. Rob gently grabs him around the waist. A bear hugging a feisty squirrel, trying not to squish it.

"I hate to say it, but maybe you guys should leave," he suggests to Band Dad, who is finally letting his frustration show.

"I think you're right," he replies, gathering up his daughter.

And I'll say this about the little girl, she felt bad for the kid. "He really wants his own bike, huh?" she tells me as she walks hers toward the gate. I think to myself, *This girl gets it.*

But before I get too hopeful about the future of race relations in America, Band Dad places his hand on Rob's shoulder, drawing him close for some sort of park-friend huddle. I imagine he's going to say "Thank you for stepping in" or "You were a big help" or "Dude, you're the best." All appropriate responses. None of which he chooses.

"There's this program in the city where kids can get free bikes," he says. "If you give me your information," he continues to our wide-eyed horror, "I can forward you the name."

The three of us stare at this man as if he has as many heads. Rob and I do a double take as the realization settles over us.

"Umm, that is not our fucking kid," I interject helpfully.

My husband is more judicious. "Yeaaaaaah," says Rob in a measured tone I recognize from frustrating work calls. "We don't actually know him."

We're still staring, unblinking, waiting for this white guy to see us, like really see us.

Band Dad looks confused at first. Then, slowly but surely, he goes all mortified. It's a summer Sunday afternoon and my husband is in a button-down and khaki pants with a stupidly expensive leather messenger bag strapped across his chest. We came to the park after brunch. My mom joined us from church. She's in her "good black pants." Sally is dressed for the 'Gram and pounding puffs out of a no-spill, BPA-free snack cup shaped like a cat. The little boy? He's ricocheting against the playground in dusty pants and dingy shoes. When Band Dad looks, like, really looks, it's clear that one of these things is not like the other.

"Oh, man. Okay, sorry. I just thought . . ."

"Nah." Rob and I shake our heads in unison. We know what he thought. It's what they all think. That we're all the same. That we can't handle our kids. That our money ain't right. That class divides don't exist for anyone but them. We continue to glare as Band Dad and his daughter bike off into the distance. Rob fixes me with a look that says all the things. *For real? I'm sick of this shit. Let's go home.* But there's still the matter of the little boy, who by now my mother is like *this close* to adopting. Major, his name was Major, we later learn. With the bike gone he looks to us for his kicks. He plops himself down by Sally and reaches into her stroller to grab a fuzzy block, twisting it in his hands before asking brightly, "Where we going next?"

Rob asks around, and Major's father is found hanging out in the permanent cluster of foldout chairs set up down the street. He comes to get his son in a cloud of smoke and cuss words that make us cringe. Frances actually starts crying a little. On the walk back, my husband bans the park for good.

"Oh right, because of all the shootings?" one of the Mamas asks when I explain that we need to pick a different park for a playdate because my husband has put the kibosh on the one just down the street. Yep, definitely. Definitely the shootings (there have been several nonfatal "incidents" in or around the green over the years). But what's really keeping us away doesn't make a bang despite hitting just as hard.

There's a strange invisibility to being a middle-class Black parent in a "transitioning" neighborhood. We are seen but not really, not fully. Like crop circles you can only truly appreciate from an aerial view that no one has time for. Instead, they make do with the stereotypes staring them in the face. It's easier. Our bodies make the loud introduction that our bachelor's degrees and bank accounts could never. Too many of the people around here see their Black neighbors as fading set pieces—remnants of the last big production, destined for the recycling bin—or worse, as suspects. Class and race are twisted up in ways that seem impossible to untangle. And it's been that way since Bloomingdale's good old days. Remember Francis de Sales Smith? One of the neighborhood's first Black homeowners? The man was an engineer, possibly one of the first Black students to graduate from the prestigious Catholic University, if my amateur Ancestry.com sleuthing is to be relied upon. But his neighbors, many of whom probably couldn't pass an algebra pop quiz with a cheat sheet, didn't care. His credentials (or his pristine front porch, his humanity) would never be greater than his color. The year was 1907; Smith's neighbors wanted to erase him—buy his house, move him out, pretend like the whole thing never happened—and white folks usually got what they wanted then. And now.

More than a century later a white dude, who's, like, *not a regular dad but a cool dad* with the names of esoteric bands stretched across his chest, assumes that because we're Black all the Black kids in the vicinity are ours—oh, and we can't afford a cheap-ass bike. And that because he is white (and good) he should swoop in with totally googleable information about free bikes for our poor bike-starved child. Also, once again, for the cheap seats—this is not our kid! That's the other thing about the class divide that is tricky. Unless you're an "our kind of people" type (generationally ensconced in the rarefied world of the "talented tenth" African American elite) then you've probably been that kid at the playground with hand-me-down shoes and a chip on your shoulder. Was it even possible for us to catch up to and run past the stereotypes? Was it even worth it? Who were we to separate ourselves from this boy?

Because in the end, white Band Dad's real crime was the crime of mistaking us for being poor. Dig into that. We were flustered and frustrated by the fact that he didn't see us on his level, the white-people level. Was the question, then, "Why does he see *us* as all the same?" or was it "Why doesn't he see that we are the same as him?" Was the anger we felt justified or was it corrupted by the constant chase of an "ideal" that America still defines as white? Put plainly, what do we want them to see when they see us?

University of Maryland sociology professor Dawn Marie Dow studies the intersection of race, class, and gender. In her book *Mothering While Black,* she uncovers the ways in which contemporary African Americans, specifically middle-class Black women, parent in response to race. Many of Dow's carefully researched assertions—about visibility, social anxiety, and racial mental labor—spoke directly to me, as if she had been listening in on the hushed late-night conversations Rob and I were having (after reading Sally one of her many Black-girl-affirming books) about how to raise our kid. But it was her categorization of different types of middle-class Black families that really flipped the switch. Dow pinpoints three categories of bougie Black folk—the Border Crossers, the Border Policers, and the Border Transcenders. Of particular interest to me were the first two. Border Crossers were parents who wanted their children to be fluent in Black culture, to have "street smarts," and to recognize the struggle. The mothers in this group were usually themselves raised by working-class parents but were now upwardly mobile. Border Policers, on the other hand, "defined African American racial identity as largely disentangled from firsthand knowledge of economic struggle." These families had most likely been upper or middle class for generations.

Border Crossers "wanted their children to be at ease in their interactions with African Americans from a range of social and economic positions" because they believed their children needed the skills "to navigate social contexts marked by different levels of racial and economic privilege," writes Dow. Basically, their kids should be "down" but also a bit uppity, depending on the company. But Border Policers wanted their kids to feel at home on the upper rungs of Black and white society and were less concerned with those at the bottom. "For these mothers, being authentically African American meant understanding the cultural, political, and historical contributions of the African American community, but they were less concerned with providing their children with direct contact with economic struggle, in part because it was less relevant to their daily lives."

Which one were we?

Setting ourselves apart from Major was never the goal; in fact, he and Frances became buds (of course). But isn't *the* goal—everyone's goal—to get to the next rung? Be the middle-class Black folks the Huxtables and the Obamas promised us existed. And if we exist, shouldn't we demand to be seen?

"That category becomes totally invisible, because it doesn't fit the stereotype," explains Shilpi Malinowski, a journalist and fellow Bloomingdale mom who literally wrote the book on our neighborhood: *Shaw, LeDroit Park & Bloomingdale in Washington, D.C.: An Oral History*. We met under "the mom tree" at Crispus Attucks Park and have remained friends ever since. Effortlessly cool in linen pants and panama hats, Shilpi's lived in the neighborhood for over a decade. As a first-generation South Asian woman raising two brown boys with a husband who immigrated to the U.S. from Poland, she has a lot to say about how class, race, nationality, and preconceived notions play out on the playground and beyond. But she's careful not to condemn. "Everyone's trying," she tells me over coffee one day as I pepper her with questions. "Everyone is trying," I repeat, like a new mantra that reminds me that not every misstep is meat off my bones.

The Invisible Population, as the two of us have now dubbed middle-class parents of color in the confines of our zip code, is only invisible to a certain type of white person whose own biases are equally concealed. They pack their prejudices along with their kid's juice boxes, either because they simply don't know any better, having previously been sequestered in homogenous spaces that didn't provide "an opportunity" to break that cycle, or perhaps "because they're willfully not seeing" the differences right in front of them, muses Shilpi.

For her book, which covers seventy years of local living, Shilpi spoke to residents of all ages, races, colors, and classes. Each subject had claimed the neighborhood as their own at one point in time. The frank conversations helped give her some perspective.

"One of the realizations I've had is that living in a truly integrated, racially diverse, and economically diverse neighborhood is really new for almost everybody," said Shilpi. The older Black folks who are here, like Miss Connie down the street from me, know this place as a majority-Black community filled with working-class families and hot nights spent on front porches. It's probably why she clung to me and Rob when we moved in before Sally was born. Why she gave our daughter her first teddy bear, knit her a pink baby quilt. Why to this day she tutors Sally in reading for an hour twice a week, sending my child home with chocolate-chip cookies wrapped in paper towels. And the "gentrifiers" in the house converted to condos next door to Miss Connie? She offers them head nods, sometimes. A lot of them came from the super white suburbs where many of Bloomingdale's original homeowners fled following *Hurd v. Hodge.* The flags they plant—yard signs promoting the liberal ideals they espouse "in this house"—don't tell the whole story of who they truly are inside.

"So even people with the best of intentions, it's like a new part of their personality that they're having to exercise. Even the people with the best of intentions end up offending somebody," Shilpi continued, which isn't to say she enjoyed being offended, she just recognized "their discomfort."

The only way to avoid the possibility of offense is to retreat— avoid rubbing elbows with anyone too different and subsequently rubbing them the wrong way. The Mamas could feel like one such hideout. Since its inception during one of the neighborhood's many waves of gentrification, the Facebook group had grown to include hundreds of moms who mostly looked, bought, thought, and voted alike. It was a giant online fishbowl floating over the ocean. Deep discussions about race and class weren't the norm.

Then lottery season happened.

For the uninitiated or those who like to maintain a semblance of sanity, the lottery season in D.C. is the brief window every year when it is socially acceptable to gamble on your preschooler's future. In Washington there are two systems (this is already sounding off, right?): public charter schools and just plain old public schools. Charter schools can feel like private schools without the price tag, with their fancy learning "philosophies," author "talks" during library time, and capstone courses for kindergarteners. In this town, the farther west and north you go, the whiter and "better" the plain old public schools get. This is according to the online peanut gallery that obsessively tracks this stuff. To get into preschool, which is universal but not guaranteed, you must enter your child's name in the lottery and rank each of your school choices from best to "This is free so therefore better than daycare."

In terms of educational prospects, Bloomingdale, right in the middle of the city, is on the cusp of good but not great. So there are two camps: the die-hard neighborhood school evangelists and "the charter school or we're moving to Bethesda, Maryland" crew. When it came time to choose a school for Sally, Rob and I hopped on the crazy train with everybody else. We did the school tours, compared test scores, weighed dual language versus Montessori, and blah, blah, blah. Just like with the Secret White Meetings, I had to make sure we (I mean Sally) didn't miss the boat. I had to be on my A game. She had to have access to everything the other kids did. On top of all that concerted cultivation—plugging into our kid like every other burned-out parent—we had the bonus of needing to take into account our Black child's safety in a public institution that had an abysmal record of doing just that.

In *Mothering While Black,* Dow calls that "invisible labor." (This is the very same increased mental load Annette Lareau didn't know what to do with.) What's more, status anxiety is a particular pain point for Black mothers because the statistics surrounding "class reproduction" (maintaining socioeconomic generational gains) for African Americans aren't great. Quoting fellow sociologist Patrick

Sharkey's work, Dow points out that nearly 50 percent of the children from middle-class Black families "experience downward mobility, as compared with 16 percent of their white middle-class counterparts." So yeah, we were slightly terrified and rightly so. The goal is to climb up the ladder, not slide down.

The debate of charter versus public was a regular one in our house. But out in the world, the issue was allegedly one only rich white saviors had to consider—stay and make the neighborhood school better with the sheer force of their presence or leave and relegate the school to the bargain basement of education.

It was lottery season when Shilpi and I sat down to chat, and just the week before, the Brookings Institution had released an eye-opening case study titled *"We All Want What's Best for Our Kids."* The forty-eight-page report examined the link between school choice and segregation through the lens of a widely popular (though often derided) online forum for bougie Washington parents, DC Urban Moms and Dads. Analyzing more than a decade's worth of posts on the school-focused threads, Brookings revealed some uncomfortable truths about how parents perceive one school versus another, how achievement is assumed when white kids are present in high numbers and the opposite goes for when they're not.

"We find that in DC Urban Moms' conversations, schools are clustered—by grade, geography, and sector, but also by the racial makeup of the student body," read the report, which everybody and I mean *everybody* was reading. "We also find that within the DC Urban Moms' forum much of the local school system is simply invisible; many schools are never discussed. Instead, a small fraction of the school system—generally, schools with a sizeable white populations and schools in wealthy or gentrifying neighborhoods—receive an outsized share of attention. The correlation between attention to a school and its racial demographics persists, even within a gentrifying neighborhood." Even when schools were high-performing—which is, like, the whole point, *right?*—if the student body had fewer white kids and was in the "wrong" neighborhood, then it didn't exist.

The study drew its title, *"We All Want What's Best for Our Kids,"* directly from a post on DC Urban Moms. That's a common refrain any parent can get behind. But exactly who is included in "we all" is another topic entirely. What shocked me most about it was that the list of marquee schools, what the report called "high-attention" schools, matched up perfectly to our own lottery list. Proximity to whiteness had once again seeped into my own parenting practices without me realizing. One of the study's goals was to explore how "members of this community think about what is 'best,' and what steps they take to acquire that 'best' for their children." How an online forum, "one that appears to be dominated by privileged parents," dissects its local school system.

"The conversations on DC Urban Moms illustrate what other research has also shown," the study concludes. "When privileged parents choose, they tend to choose segregation."

Shilpi, whose two sons attend their local public school, has seen that particular dynamic play out in her kids' classrooms, which, as it so happens, are incredibly diverse, like a PS Benetton. There is no majority there, which is also to say white kids don't outnumber all the other kids. An active parent from preschool on, Shilpi watched as all the children in her older son's class thrived academically and socially. She also watched as many of the white parents she knew in the beginning slowly started trickling out to the charters or the burbs. It was clear to her the exodus wasn't about achievement, not just because of what she could see with her own eyes but from what she heard with her own ears.

"When my oldest son was in pre-K, a couple of white parents explicitly said to me that they were uncomfortable with the small number of white kids at the school," Shilpi tells me. "They say that . . . to *me*." File this under another one of the bizarre interactions that happen to the Invisible Population. Shilpi is Indian. She is not white and can't pass for white. And yet white parents, who presumably know her well enough to bond over shared social class and values, "see what they want to see." They want only to see the connection; they don't want to see anything else (namely race) that might make said connection more complicated. It reminded me of Band Dad and his aggressive not-seeing. Obviously not everyone is like this. Shilpi has plenty of awesome non–*sliiightly* racist mom and dad friends across the spectrum. But those who are like that, they stand out in one's mind. Also, what exactly is she supposed to do with white folks' racial disquiet? The distress they place in her lap?

"It's so hard for me. You can see their kid is thriving. This person is just uncomfortable with being a racial minority, because they've never been one before and they don't know how to do it. *We* do it all the time, but they can go their whole lives without having to experience being a minority. I don't know how to make them more comfortable."

I knew that feeling too, of trying to be comfortable with the uncomfortable. We'd been going back and forth about school choice in the Super Cool Moms since citywide applications had opened that winter. Who went to what open house? Who liked this charter versus that charter? Was dual language a thing? Did it matter? And if so, would *I* have to start learning Mandarin too? Was it bad to only consider schools that were on your route to work? Or was it actually genius? But the topic that rarely came up was the public school a ten-minute walk east. It was an afterthought at best, at worst a clear indication of what we really thought about the neighborhood. That we were in it but not of it, not really, anyway. Even Leah, bleeding heart that she was, bemoaned the impending doom of having to move to milquetoast Upper Northwest "if we don't lottery into our top choices." But move she would. Was our local school a pariah or an elephant? It was the last elementary school standing after one building after another shuttered. The Brookings study would classify it as a "low-attention" school, with a largely Black population, *meh,* but rising test scores and a building in need of sprucing. But the principal was a Black woman with two decades of experience. There was a community garden, and the kids were being taught to "regulate" their emotions by breathing into an imaginary balloon. No one was talking about it. We ranked it twelfth out of twelve schools.

The angst over where to send Sally was familiar territory. We'd gone through the same agonizing process when we'd started looking for daycares a few years before, once it became clear that our multigenerational fantasy was just that. All the big-name places cost as much as our rent. Remember the Cognac from our pre-kid days? The binge drinking bout brought on by the high price of childcare before we even had a kid to take care of? We sobered up quickly. The Mamas provided a steady stream of information about nanny shares and vetted daycares—all of which were way out of my preferred price range of "affordable." So when I passed a Baptist church on my way to work one day and saw a banner depicting smiling children who didn't appear to be the victims of abuse, I dug my phone out of my purse and dialed the number.

"Is it clean and do they speak enough English for you to piece together what she did all day?" texted Sofia from the West Coast when I told her I'd found the needle in the haystack but was unsure since no one I knew (code for none of the Mamas, code for no white folks) was talking about it. The place was run by a triumvirate of women—Filipino, Ethiopian, and Black—who regularly praised Sally for being smarter than your average toddler. "Sally talks so good!" they'd tell us. Rob often wondered if we were holding her back in some way, seeing as how we were paying half what everyone else was. The real difference was more obvious. All the kids at the center were Black except for a little white boy named Rohan, whose parents biked in every morning. But they sang the same mind-numbing songs, ate the same paste, and practiced peeing in the same potties as the other kids at the fancier daycares. We didn't need a brand-name experience.

"She's two," I explained as if my husband didn't already know that.

"I know that," he said. "I just want to make sure we're not short-changing her, trying to save some coins." I was steadfast, always coming back to Sof's advice. Sally was clean(ish) at the end of the day, and more than that, she was adored for those eight hours by women who looked like her and among kids who looked like her. We never wondered about the messages she was being sent subliminally, unlike during that one week when our center's air conditioner broke down and we had to send Sally to a brand-name daycare temporarily. Every teacher there was Black, but Sally was the only little Black girl in her room—a Scandinavian wonderland of wooden toys and matching mini furniture. "I hate the idea of her thinking Black people are just like in service or something," said Rob as we walked out the door. I nodded, saying a little prayer for the AC.

Still, whenever the topic of daycares came up, I always added the caveat that our center was "lo-fi." There was no iPad for morning sign-in, no daily photo collage of your child's "sensory play," no "extras." It was like I was apologizing for the place, preempting any "judgment by the cover." But what other daycare scheduled a beloved yearly field trip to the UniverSoul Circus? What other day-care had a Ms. Etenesh, who for thirty dollars would braid my little girl's cloud of curls? We were good. But no one else from the neighborhood (save my Black friend Lynne) sent their kids there, despite my occasional plugs for a place that "loved the kids for half the price."

By lottery season I'd had plenty of practice looking past the bells and whistles. I knew the sweet sound of toddlers laughing unbidden or singing the ABC's or reciting the Lord's Prayer without having any clue who said Lord was. It was about the people. And yet I said a Hail Mary before hitting "view my results" on Sally's lottery application. Had we won? Or had we lost?

The jury was still out when Shilpi and I grabbed coffee. Our "numbers" were abysmal. Sally had been waitlisted everywhere but our friendly neighborhood school—the one we'd listed at the bottom. We could either spend the next six months hoping that one of the "better" schools offered her a slot for the upcoming year, or we could say, "Fuck it," and go all in. Does anyone want to say, "Fuck it," when it comes to their kid's education? Why did walking up the street to enroll feel akin to throwing caution to the wind? I was trying to get past that psychological roadblock when the Mamas once again stepped in to help put things in perspective. The group was capable of both pushing me into an anxiety-fueled leap and bringing me back down to earth.

Of course, the school debate was ripe for Facebook. One of the original Mamas, an out-and-proud public-school parent, posted an impassioned plea attempting to convince all the good "upper-middle-class white parents" to consider our local elementary school. It was a deeply personal story about the lottery and what it meant to her. How "winning" and "losing" shouldn't be the goal when it comes to your kid's education. She quoted the Brookings report about white flight from public education, outlined school demographics, defined what "at risk" meant. It was loooong. It was thoughtful. It was fair. And, child, if it ain't piss me the hell off.

Sure, it was a start. She was in the right place, as they say, trying to assuage the fears, assumptions, and misconceptions that contribute to educational inequities. But in doing so her story still completely ignored an entire swath of the neighborhood, namely parents that looked like me. The Blacks. The hot-button issues brought up—test scores, performance, growth—were all the same benchmarks Rob and I (and every other middle-class Black parent we knew) had been grappling with. We wanted to support public education but didn't want our kid "to be the experiment," because we also knew that white activism can be seasonal, and when the dust settles, white people always have more exits available to them. None of that nuance was in this post. Instead, it read—intentionally or not—like a glossy time-share brochure meant to calm white fear of the unknown. Once again, class and race got Hulk-smashed together. Once again, *we* weren't seen as the same—or even in the same room. The Invisible Population, who, for reasons that reached far beyond what was trendy, were wary of the public school system too. But our concerns weren't theirs and therefore were of no concern. As it read, it was up to the affluent white parents of the neighborhood to lift our local school out of obscurity. It called for "unity." Unity? *Pfft.* Among whom? The post racked up an insane number of virtual high fives, and I just about died inside.

"Did you see this shit on the Facebook group," I texted Monica, a Black mom friend who'd just moved a few blocks from us and who believed wholeheartedly in our neighborhood school. Mon texted back the nervous emoji. We both knew that this "important conversation" could go off the rails with just one mention of "those people." After several more rage texts from me, Monica responded thoughtfully because I couldn't. All the pent-up pressure built from trying to raise this Black child around these white people who, according to this post (okay, not just this post but *everything*), saw themselves as saviors was giving me migraines.

"Our community has affluent families of color as well, who are excluded or ignored. This isn't just about rich white and poor Black families," she wrote, emphasizing that "affluent" Black families, of which there were many in a neighborhood with a median home price of $800,000, often felt "invisible" and that "*all* families" should be recruited to invest in the local school. Surprisingly, no one got offended. If anything, folks were listening. I chimed in that we had to stop conflating class and race. Shilpi talked about erasure. A Latinx mom said she was once mistaken as her fairer-skinned son's nanny. Someone posted a link to *The New York Times*'s *Nice White Parents* podcast on race and school choice. It was a moment. Not a kumbaya moment per se. But *a* moment.

The likes and replies were still rolling in when Shilpi and I sat down for breakfast burritos to talk shop. I spent most of our hour together yakking with my mouth half full about the push and pull in our lives that white mothers would never understand. How I wasn't sure they really wanted to. How I didn't want to be the Great Explainer—jumping on every microaggression in the Mamas group or every slip of the tongue at the playground—but I couldn't let things slide either. What kind of Black person would that make me if I did? Wouldn't I render myself invisible in the process?

All the lottery foolishness made me think back to Major, whose playground shenanigans put us on blast by revealing exactly what some folks think about us despite all our middle-class trappings. I never saw him again. The shootings calmed down for a bit, the community had a meeting, and Rob's ban on the park was temporarily lifted. But the place was still across the street from "the condos," so there were still plenty of opportunities for culture clashes, and they weren't always Black and white.

Once, I was there with my mom friend Lynne, who I all but accosted after spotting her on the street with a brown baby whose cheeks were undeniably her own. Lynne is the kind of nice that throws you off. It's genuine to the point of supernatural. But homegirl does not play about her kids. On this particular afternoon a bigger boy in swim trunks and no T-shirt, who could've been a Major, shoved her son backward down a steep slide on purpose.

"Where is your mother?" Lynne asked the boy pointedly. He shrugged his shoulders. She then marched him out of the play-ground to a group of women listening to the radio at the picnic tables nearby. "He's done," Lynne told the woman who claimed him, and then she returned to her own kids. I watched from my side of the gate wide-eyed and high-key impressed. *Okay, Lynne.* Never once would I have done that. I don't have the confrontation gene and, more important, I can't fight worth a damn, especially toe-to-toe with a mom from "the condos." And yes, I assumed she'd want to fight. Which is exactly what I was thinking when said mom stomped over with her son in tow to ask *me* what had happened. *My name is Bennett!*

"So what he do?" she demanded while Lynne was conveniently busy on the opposite side of the playground near the swings, leav-ing me to handle the situation alone should we have a situation on our hands. I put my big-girl panties on and told her that he'd pushed a younger boy hard. She nodded her head.

"Okay, okay. Because *she* just came over talking about he couldn't play anymore," said the mom, thrusting her chin in Lynne's direc-tion. "I mean, this is a public space."

"Right, right. He was just being a bit too rough, I think."

"Ummhmm. I mean, I expect it from them, you know," she said, not having to explain who she was referring to. "But us?"

Once again, I was left contemplating who "us" was. How race and class and money and made-up shit separate us in ways we see and ways we don't—or maybe we do and we're just too lazy to break out a magnifying glass. How "us" is up to who holds the power, who lets you in and who is behind the gate. I'd been invisible to *them,* but who was invisible to *us*?

CHAPTER 7

Your Mom's Vagina

One of the biggest bonuses of the Mamas, particularly the Super Cool Moms spin-off, was that it provided a reliable vent for the vagaries of women on the verge of nervous breakdowns. The group chat was like a ticker tape of what ticked us off about being moms. Top of the list: our own moms.

When the pandemic began, several women escaped to their childhood homes with the juicy carrot of free childcare dangling on a string. What they all got was something different. Mira was ready to call it quits after months of hiding in her childhood bedroom from her mom, Mimi, the retired grandma ninja. "It's the only place I can relax," she explained of closing the door and diving onto her teenage twin bed. Carly sympathized. "Two weeks is my max," she said after a tumultuous fourteen days that nearly damaged her relationship with her mother beyond repair. I was struggling too.

"I'm just seriously hoping that when/if I'm a grandmother I will not be insane. But that's doubtful," I wrote, trying to work out my own problems in one hundred characters or less. "All of us (including our children) have to survive our mothers."

Surviving our mothers. It's a baptism that can feel a lot like drowning.

The accidental advantage of becoming a mother "later in life" is that you've already had plenty of practice parenting your old-ass parents. See, you waited so long to have your own kid that your mom is just like "Fine, then!" and takes matters into her own hands, becoming the baby you've been too slow to provide. No one tells you about this secret bonus level of *Adulthood: The Video Game* until you're already deep in the trenches, collecting gold coins you can't spend anywhere but in therapy.

Case in point: my mother's vagina. Trust me, this is going somewhere.

Not long before I got pregnant with Sally, I saw my mom's cooch more in the space of a year than anyone without a medical license. It was . . . humbling. It was also the beginning of my own birthing process, yanking me from one reality to the next.

I saw her vadge in the hospital, at home, on a toilet, in the shower, and once in my best friend's guest bedroom. I saw it by accident, in passing, sort of on purpose, and because it was propped up for my inspection. I've. Seen. My. Mother's. Vagina.

Judging by the lack of a ticker-tape parade, I guess it's simply understood that at some point in life you will be forcibly transformed from a woman who has only seen her mother's vageen during the blissfully forgotten trauma of her own birth to one who sees it when her eyes are open. I was woefully unprepared. But can you study for this test of maturity? Flash-card your way into being okay with getting flashed on a daily basis? Probably not. The trick is to suck it up and pretend like everything is normal until it is. That was the lesson my mother nearly dying from necrotizing fasciitis taught me about parenting—fake it until it no longer freaks you the fuck out.

Day 0

I should be ashamed to admit that when "the call" came my finger hovered not so briefly over the "ignore" button. It was one of my four aunts on the line. Each is a distinct brand of Black woman for whom poems, love songs, and memes are made. They get their hair done on Saturdays, they only smoke where you can't see, and their *ummhmms* can snatch your very soul. It was Auntie Barbara, the responsible one, so I pressed "answer" despite being in the middle of a very important podcast about Kylie Jenner's lips. "Did you know that your mother . . ." Auntie started out and I immediately hit pause, not knowing that the feeling of being interrupted would last the rest of the year.

There were long stretches between Auntie's sentences, as if whatever was wrong was too big for her to get out in one breath. "She's just . . . acting funny . . . And she . . . took these pills." Somehow, though, I was still annoyed. It was just like Frances to scare people half to death when everything was really fine. Like the time she left thirteen-year-old me at the port in San Pedro and, assuming she'd been executed by wayward pirates, I boarded the ferry to Catalina alone and with the singular knowledge that my mother was dead. When I arrived at my best island friend's house two hours later, her mother told me the truth. I wasn't an orphan after all; turns out Frances got a parking ticket and was trying to talk her way out of it. This was probably just that.

"Should I come home?" I asked Auntie Barbara, testing out the role of a dutiful daughter—you know, running the lines but not really wanting the part. I was hoping Auntie would beg me off with a "Don't worry about it, we'll handle it. I just wanted you to know." But this was my mother.

"That'd probably be a good idea," she said. I landed at LAX the next afternoon.

When I poked my head into Frances's bedroom, which had once belonged to my grandmother and before that my great-grandmother, the smell of murder slapped me in the face like so much CK One on a horny fourteen-year-old. It was musty and rancid—badissy gone bad. My mother was sweating as if she were being burned at the stake, the imaginary fire just reaching her toes. Her hair had gone wild. Her breathing more so. She looked like a sea witch, in sagging boxer briefs and a soaking wet shredded tank that read CATALINA ISLAND REGGAE FEST '88. And she'd been like this for five days.

Counting backward, it dawned on me that my mother and I hadn't spoken in more than a week. Frances lived by herself in a house filled with ghosts and didn't want to bother anyone. Auntie B, doing her regular check-ins of Grandmommy's house—which technically hadn't been Grandmommy's house since she had died three months earlier—found her big sister like this. She was found. This both enraged me and validated my life choices. Immediately I mentally patted myself on the back. Thank God I was legally bound to another person who, if anything, wouldn't let me rot for a week, at least not without having to answer to the police. But then again, my mother supposedly had a grown and responsible daughter who should have protected her from the same. So what exactly did that say about me? Mercifully, there was no time to answer that.

"Oh, Lena," said Frances with an unsteady rasp when she spotted me hovering apprehensively at the bedroom door. "You didn't have to come."

The plan was to go to the ER the next morning, because Auntie wanted whatever Chinese muscle relaxants Frances had been taking for joint pain (another saga) to flush out of her system.

"She's been acting so crazy," Auntie whispered to me in the hallway. "I think it's the pills. I don't want them to commit her."

"I'm sorry? What?" Apparently, Frances's newly erratic behavior (twitching, paranoia, demanding citrus fruit at odd hours) could land her in the psych ward if we showed up at the hospital with her. So Auntie, a registered nurse, wanted to wait it out lest we find ourselves in really deep. I did not pack for this level of seriousness. That night I went to bed pretending as if everything would be fine in the morning. We'd go to the hospital; they'd diagnose my mother with Old Lady Disease No. 9 and send us home with an antibiotic that would clear it up in five to seven business days. The end. My mother shook me out of that dream well before the sun came up.

"I need a bath. And some orange slices with a little bit of honey," she whispered to me, face floating over mine at four in the morning.

"What? No. Ma, go back to sleep. We're going to hospital in like two hours," I answered groggily.

"Lena, run the water!" She was already halfway to the bathroom, stripping off clothes as she went. Vagina sighting number one. Afterward I had to get Frances dressed, because for some reason her arms no longer worked. Vagina sighting number two. Later, when the ER nurse got a good look at Frances's now elephant-sized and bright red right arm, she looked me in the eyes and said, "Things are going to start happening quickly." In seconds, a swarm of blue scrubs surrounded my mother to cut off the clothes it took me fifteen minutes to get her into. Vagina sighting number three. A rotating roster of specialists came in every hour until midnight. By the time they told us what was wrong (cellulitis, septicemia, and deep vein thrombosis, to start) and began using fun euphemisms like "not life sustaining," there was no use counting.

Day 1

The first night we spent in the hospital was predictably terrible. But not for the reasons a decent human being might think. You know how the surest way to win any talent show is to sing a song about

Jesus, because no one can boo the guy who died on the cross or, by proxy, the tone-deaf fool in gold lamé screeching "Amazing Grace" off-key? It's as if everyone in the audience reflexively decides to be better people—at least for the length of the song. Using that same sympathy, you'd think that when my mom got sick, I'd be able to tap into that natural spring of involuntary goodness—if only temporarily. I thought so too.

As it turns out, caregiving is a muscle. One that was basically atrophying from neglect. I was terrible at it, particularly when enraged. What pissed me off the most was that Frances had sort of done this to herself. She'd been feeling sick for weeks, but due to an aversion to doctors and an affinity for storefront acupuncturists, my mother just got some "pills" and a few shots in the arm from her "needle lady." Then, when her health took a real nosedive—her arm turned beet red, she started hallucinating—she went as far as an ER waiting room. For all of five minutes. "It was packed in there and I didn't feel like sitting for hours," she explained to me in the ICU later. I was livid. Terrified. But mostly livid. So even as my mother lay in her hospital bed, tubes sprouting from her body as if it were a potato left too long on a windowsill, I rolled my eyes and snapped at her more times than any good person should admit. How could she do this to herself? To me? To us?

Plus, she kept asking for things—ice, water, more ice, the shades drawn, the TV turned up, the TV turned down—and always just as I sat down to get comfortable for a night in the pleather chairs. "Okay, what else?!" It was endless!

"I'm trying to balance wanting to murder her and swaddle her," I confessed to my childhood best friend, Gina, who'd hopped on the 105 at 4 P.M., when I had called in tears. "Something is, like, seriously wrong with her!" That, my friends, is friendship. Diving into rush hour in L.A. with zero hesitation. That is love. Gina was better at this caregiving thing than me.

"Let's do option number two for now, dude," she said.

I was doing this all wrong and I knew it, but the pressure of being the person in charge of another was whittling me down to a sullen teenager instead of sharpening me into a sensible adult. I was severely lacking in whatever "strong Black woman" superpower was supposed to kick in when times got *Good Times* rough.

This, of course, was before we knew how sick she really was. When we thought that tomorrow we'd be out of the ICU and onto a telemetry floor and then down to the next floor and down and down until we were back in the parking lot and this whole nightmare would be forgotten. But before that fantasy was crushed, I eventually got the chance to breathe and all that came out was fire.

"I can't sleep here," I fumed when the clock got to 9 P.M. By then we'd been in the hospital for twelve hours and had seen as many doctors. She had a blood clot, they knew, and something else they didn't. "This is so friggin' uncomfortable."

"No problem, baby girl," she answered, smiling. "I'll be all right." And her sweetness made me even angrier, because obviously she wasn't all right, none of this was all right and there was no one else to take charge but me. Couldn't she see how ridiculous this situation was?

As my mind spiraled into the darkest recesses of what could happen, outwardly all I could be was a giant dick. I couldn't resist the urge; it was a familiar crutch in the face of fear and Frances's particular brand of foolishness. We had been here before.

"What the hell is Bengay fever?" I shouted through the phone, thinking the louder my voice the more in control of it I'd be.

"Dengue, Lena, dengue," Frances corrected with a weak tremble. This was years before the necrotizing fasciitis. It was late on Christmas Eve in 2012 when I realized I hadn't heard from my mom, who was living on Saint Croix then. We hadn't talked since I had "got snippy" with her a few days earlier. When I noticed zero missed calls with her name on them, I phoned her up to apologize by asking if she got the present we spent a small fortune shipping.

My mother answered while on her way out of the hospital parking lot. She'd gotten sick with dengue fever, a viral infection spread by mosquitoes common in "the tropics" that's like the flu. There is no vaccine or "cure." You just get over it with rest, fluids, and Tylenol. Still, she sounded like an old lady and not at all like the fearless woman who moved to Saint Croix "just because" on her sixtieth birthday. I was scared, so naturally I got mad at her.

"What do you mean the emergency room?!"

Because I'm my mother's daughter, fear manifests itself as a controlled "So what now?" and never "Oh my God, the sky is falling!" It's a mask that, despite being rigid and uncomfortable, gets the job done. But if your mom's sick, like really really sick, not only is the sky falling, the earth is crumbling beneath your feet. It's the end of days. And when you can't get to her in time with an umbrella or a jet pack, the guilt kills your gas. Yelling seemed like a good alternative.

After the dengue fever debacle, I had vowed to be more attentive, more present, more aware of the "Frances situation," as Rob liked to call my mother's modus operandi. But years passed as they do. Frances, like so many parents who live miles away from their kids, began to take on a kind of omnipresence. She was there in the cheesy memes she posted on Facebook, in her random emails, over the occasional unreadable text, and in the reflection in the mirror. I heard her on the phone and in my own voice. She was always there, if not always right in front of me.

That's another reason I was so angry in the ICU a few years later. It was classic "It's not you, it's me." I knew I'd been failing her but didn't know how to be there for her. Sure, I'd showed up, which according to inspirational quotes is half the battle, but really that ain't shit. All that did was shine a spotlight on how much time I'd wasted in the years between. I should have been doomsday prepping instead of daydreaming about my perfect little life in D.C., which was so far removed from everything my mother was going through in Los Angeles. It was easy to explain away my anxiety as anger when I physically couldn't step in and be the daughter she needed. But now I was standing right beside her and still didn't know how to be that person. I remember an orderly asking me, "Is this your grandmother?" And I was horrified. Did she really look *that* fucking old? Or did I look that young and ill-prepared?

Day 21

It's 4:30 in the morning when my pillow gets pissed off. A second later the whole bed comes alive like a fresh zombie, jolting my body awake from a deathlike sleep. A squinty glance at my phone confirms the worst: "St. Jerome ICU." Fuck.

I brace myself, which means I suck in all the air that'll fit in my lungs and then squeeze my abs tight as if prepping for a wrecking ball. This is obviously how ninjas do it, and whenever I'm terrified my first instinct is to go full superhero. Right now, I'm beyond scared. A stranger is probably calling to inform me of my new status as a miserable orphan. *Mrs. Dyer,* I imagined Nurse Reaper would say in a dispassionate staccato, *I have bad news.* Yep, my mother is definitely dead. And I'm about to hear the worst while half sleeping on the hard twin bed in the "little room" at Grandmommy's house, which coincidentally was also the scene of my underwhelming freshman-year deflowering. Twin beds are the root of all evil.

"Hello?" I answer shakily.

"Lena?" Frances croaks into the phone like a little bird. *Okay, good, definitely not dead.*

"I really want a drink of water," she says, and it's alarming how fast fear can morph into fury.

Did I mention it was 4:30 in the morning? That I was on a hard-ass bed topped with an ancient and useless foam egg crate? That for the last three weeks I couldn't swallow the malignant lump in my throat and called my own doctor in a panic? That I had lockjaw from stress? That the last-minute trip to check on Frances had turned into Family and Medical Leave? That my mother was so sick but bafflingly still alive that her doctors nicknamed her "the Termi-nator"? That she had necrotizing fasciitis, the rare flesh-eating bac-teria? That she'd had two surgeries already and another one was coming? That none of this should've been happening because my mom was only sixty-four, which wasn't old old, just sort of old? And I most definitely wasn't old enough to deal?

I let out a minute-long woosah to keep myself from exploding.

"I know, Ma, but you can't have it," I say, trying to be as patient with the sixty-four-year-old her as I know she'd been with the six-year-old me. "Remember you have surgery in the morning? You can't eat or drink anything."

"But I'm so thirsty," she answers back, in a tiny voice that sounds as if she's shouting through a faulty megaphone a million miles away.

"You can't have water right now. Tomorrow, okay?"

"They're starving me!" She shouts as loud as her beat-up lungs can manage before remembering the nurse who's holding the phone to her ear because her infected arm can't manage it. "Lena," she's stage-whispering now. "They. Are. Starving. Me."

"They're definitely not doing that. I am positive that's not what's happening."

"It's been several weeks, and I haven't had any nourishment, any food."

"I know what nourishment means, Ma," I say, frustration growing. "You've had an IV and a feeding tube and you usually get water," I tell her, ticking off just a small fraction of the things currently keeping her alive.

"I don't!"

"You do," I say, wondering how much longer I can keep this up, marveling at the patience I've managed to squeeze from some newly discovered spring. This was one of the moments (and there had been many) where I felt the shift. This was not at all how my 2016 was supposed to go. I had plans that did not include pretend-planning my mother's funeral in case things went exactly how her doctors said they would. I was supposed to be reveling in newlywedness—cooking my hot-out-the-oven husband whatever retro recipe ensured that this commitment we'd made would stick. I was thinking a quiche. And we wanted to finally buy a house—oh, and maybe start saving money for said house. And maybe a baby? What I wasn't supposed to be doing was adulting this damn hard. My mother was supposed to be a fuzzy constant on the other side of the continent that I didn't have to think about until we called with the news of her much-lusted-after grandchild. Perhaps in a year or three. She wasn't supposed to be my responsibility—yet. But she didn't know that. So here we were fighting over a thimble-sized paper cup of water.

"Lena, I haven't had any wa—"

"You have, Mommy. Do you really think I'd let you die of thirst? Of all the things: thirst?" I laugh. She doesn't.

Very little is funny about necrotizing fasciitis and septicemia. These are life-threatening bullies that don't give a shit about what the fully grown and gainfully employed only daughter of the crazy lady who puts all her medical faith in "healing white light" has planned. Life just happens. Because if not me, then who? I was Frances's person. Her one and only. Her first and last. Her longest relationship. She liked to call me her "501c3" (she meant 401k), and the pressure was heavy on my chest, but I was learning to carry it without letting it crush me.

Once, when I was on my way to grab lunch in the hospital cafeteria, Frances looked at me and said, "You know you're my favorite, right?"

And because I'm a bratty asshole, I answered, "Well it's not like I had a choice."

And because my mother is a much better feminist than me, she shot back, "I did."

In the face of my mother's choices, specifically to let zygote me take up residence in her womb, who was I to complain when it came time to finally pay the rent?

Suddenly I was the daughter who knew how to handle stuff like medical records, insurance, death directives, and lawsuits. I was the one who eventually wouldn't think twice about asking, "How long have you been bleeding from there?" when presented with bloody toilet paper. Was it more than I could handle? The short answer is "yes and no," but the journey between those points on the map was rough. You don't go from being tear-soaked to take-charge in an Uber ride to the emergency room, but you can't take too long either. I got the hang of it once I realized no one was coming to save us but me.

"But, Lena, I'm soooo thirsty." Now she's crying. And my hardened heart is breaking.

"I know this really sucks. Tomorrow we'll have all the water! Just not tonight, okay?"

"Okay," she says finally, and all I can think about is drifting back to sleep before spending another long day on pins and needles. *So this is it, huh?* This is what it's like to be heartbroken, awed, and exhausted by a powerless person's determination to fight the Man, i.e., me, by any means necessary? Basically, this is what it's like to parent a toddler. I had no clue then how anyone did that without going insane.

"But for right now"—my mother cuts into my reverie—"I'll just have a few sips."

Day 30

Frances is "communing with the spirits" by emitting a string of guttural sounds. I didn't have the heart to tell her how not PC this was. Because when your mother's body has been ravaged by a flesh-eating bacteria you previously believed existed only on *Grey's*, you forgive her her racism. You take alive over woke any day. You let her chant something vaguely Native American–sounding despite being pretty sure she has not a clue what she is actually saying or if said words are in fact words, because she deserves it. She's made it this far.

Plus, there's a butchy nurse yanking bleach-filled surgical sponges out of your mother's split-open right arm—the arm her doctors told you she might lose—like a magician's never-ending handkerchief. And for some mystical reason the chanting is helping. So you silently join in, hoping that the "words" coming out of her mouth loosely translate to, "Apologies, Great Spirit, I know we're only like a thirty-sixth Cherokee on our great-grandmother's side but please, please don't let her die today."

Frances still won't admit it, but we've been in the hospital a month, currently prepping for her umpteenth surgery and praying to whoever's in charge, because she's single. Single in the sense that she goes through life alone. Because she refuses to hold on to things besides me. Because she approaches life like a Choose Your Own Adventure book instead of a thoughtful undertaking that requires planning or at the very least an email address that isn't just a bunch of numbers and letters thrown together.

If we're lucky, as we get older our mothers become more like older sisters, or at least that was my dream before this nightmare. They're the women who make you feel grounded but don't weigh you down. You tell each other your secrets and hope for sound advice, which is why after my grandmother died my mother put off moving back to Saint Croix to run a salad stand for at-risk youths (seriously). She asked me what I thought, and I told her she should stay put. Instead of hightailing it back to her happy place, she waited in Los Angeles to "figure things out" and caught a life-threatening illness in the process. So maybe this was all *my* fault. My obsession with plotting, knowing all the things before you make a move, had precipitated her downfall.

"I mean, what's your plan? Not the salad plan, woman," I hounded when she told me she wanted to go back to the island.

"I don't know. I just want to get there and see. There's abundance everywhere. I can make money anywhere. I just need to go." I convinced her to stay, and within months she was in the hospital. I told myself it wasn't on me that Frances never takes care of herself, that at least she got sick in the actual United States and not on the island so many miles from home. But whose home was I thinking about?

During the three years my mother lived on Saint Croix I visited a grand total of once. Back then Frances still occupied a hazy "Oh yeah, my mom retired in the Caribbean" space in my brain that lulled me into complacency like so many warm ocean waves. Okay, fine, I'd effectively let myself off the hook. Who needs to check on their mother when she hangs at the beach all day? "She's *fiiiiine*," I'd sing whenever anyone asked. When I finally got there to check on her like a good only child, I wanted to scream—but the rooster in Frances's backyard kept drowning me out. In the MASH game of life, my mother had landed irrefutably on "shack." She was living in a leaning "one" bedroom without a real address. It was located off the side of the road and across the "street" from the island's sole

AARP office. This is not hyperbole. When I asked what to tell my taxi driver at the airport she said, and I quote, "Over by the AARP office." Her place had occasional electricity and constant chickens. She described one of her neighbors thusly: "Weeeell, I'm pretty sure she's a prostitute." I spent one night on her twin bed propped up on cinder blocks before demanding that we go to a hotel, unable to confront the stark reality that living by the seat of your swimsuit well into your sixties wasn't romantic, brave, or "the dream," it was fucking dangerous.

Day 40

"Dude, you know there was a serial killer that lived like three blocks from here, right?" Gina delivers this disturbing news as we pull into the busted driveway of Grandmommy's very empty Spanish-style stucco house in South Central. Now it looked haunted.

"Wait, what?" *No, I did not know there was a mass murderer who probably went to the same McDonald's as us.*

"Yeah, man," says Gina with the Explorer still running and my hand on the passenger-side door, "he killed, like, twenty women in as many years. Probably more. Left them dead as shit in alleys all around here. They *just* caught his ass."

"Please tell me he wasn't Black . . ."

"Dude . . . look where we are."

And where were we exactly?

We were at my grandmother's house, which was no longer my grandmother's house. Our family's matriarch had died that December. Now my mother was living there alone and in mourning. But actually, she wasn't. My mother was in the hospital. That was where she lived now. After more than a month I had to admit that. So whose home was it?

Technically I lived there now, curled up on a stiff twin bed in the "little room" because I refused to sleep on the mattress my grand-mother died on, despite Auntie's reassurance that "the sheets were clean," or even step my big toe into the room where my mother almost died, which also happened to be the last two hundred square feet my great-grandmother ever saw. This place was filled with ghosts—Andrews women who'd been swallowed up by it but refused to leave—and now I was one of them.

There is a hallowed history of women taking care of each other in my family. At seventy-five, my grandmother took out a home equity loan to build a third bedroom for my ninety-five-year-old great-grandmother, who at that point kept forgetting her name and escaping from the old folks' home. Watching the two of them together was humbling. One tired woman dressing the other, brushing her silver-spun hair into a low bun and cooking her what-ever she liked. Two old ladies arguing about whether the grits had been made "the right way." Two women fighting to exist in the same space. Frenchie, my grandmother, could be mean. Nonny, my great-grandmother, could be meaner. Grandmommy called her mother "m'dear" on most days and "Mother Dear" only when she was frustrated. Once, my Auntie Leta, the fun one, told me that she'd asked Grandmommy why she put up with Nonny's outbursts over the years—some of which could be legendary. My grand-mother's response was simple: "That's my mother."

When Nonny died in her bedroom one Christmas morning and Frenchie was summarily alone, Auntie Barbara convinced Frances to move from her beloved Saint Croix to help take care of my grandmother, who suddenly, with no one to take care of, was show-ing her own age. My mother agreed and moved back within weeks. My grandmother subsequently complained about her third daugh-ter's twisted island hair so much my mom eventually got it straight-ened at the beauty college down the street.

"I'm the black sheep," she whispered to me over the phone once, convinced that everyone (read: her sisters) was talking about her. "I can't do anything right! I can't be myself here."

Unsure of how to comfort her I said, "Just stop messing around with your hair on the couch, Grandmommy can't stand that."

Then Grandmommy died and Frances got sick. Now it was my turn to write my name down in the Big Book of Black Women. I wasn't exempt from the tradition just because I lived a few miles away from the Obamas and a few thousand away from my family. I was on deck and resented it, mainly because I felt so small compared to the five-foot giants that had come before me. How could I stand next to them in the Andrews tradition of taking care of our own when I'd played hooky on being the dutiful daughter for so long?

Our little haunted house on Eighty-eighth and Normandie terrified me because it made me stretch, and it comforted me because being inside felt like a tight squeeze. Either way, one thing was clear—it shaped me more than I realized then. It was refuge, base camp, and training ground. Run by women for women. When I walked inside that night, still jumpy from Gina's tale of the Grim Sleeper—that was the serial killer's name, by the way—I was alone but not. I would never be truly alone. The walls still reverberated with the ten-minute lectures Nonny delivered to anyone who dared "disrespect" her house by eating on a paper plate, the sighs Grandmommy would let out when I slept past 8 A.M. during summer vacations; the smoke of fried fish cheeks lingered; there was a sweet scent wafting from vases filled with long-dead funeral flowers that the aunties refused to throw away.

In Alice Walker's *In Search of Our Mothers' Gardens,* the author, whose work cluttered our house when I was a child, wrote, "How simple a thing it seems to me that to know ourselves as we are, we must know our mothers' names." And the inspirational quote often stops there if you're searching online. But the rest of Walker's thought continues, "Yet, we do not know them. Or if we do, it is only the names we know and not the lives." I was knee-deep in those lives. Padding from room to room when I wasn't at the hospital. Man, I hated that house where so many lives had ended, but I needed that house where so many had been lived. It described who I was, who I wasn't, and who I wanted to be.

Day 55

"So, you're the . . . ?"

I'd been waiting for this morning's nurse to ask "the question." And after nearly three months at my mother's bedside, I should have been able to fill in the blank. It was the same every day. Each new stranger arriving to poke and prod my mother's exhausted body wanted to know just who I was to this woman. The question came easy and often. The answer, however, did not. I'm her daughter, obviously. But in the hospital, I was more than that. Or perhaps I became more *of* that.

I'd made a ritual of avoiding asking myself the question. Every day before the elevator closed the doors on the worry-free existence outside the hospital, I'd distract myself. Scrolling past the well-meaning but maddening texts, drowning my hands with an ice-cream scoop of foamy sanitizer, widening my eyes to tighten the leaky emotions before the elevator dinged open and I stepped into the ICU. *Will I get to be her daughter today or will I have to be her mother?*

Would I wear my "Whatever it is you like" cap as Frances, newly extubated and drunk on power, barked throaty orders to close those drapes and find a "nice fruit salad" somewhere? Or would I strap on my "Yep, I'm definitely the one in charge" helmet to sign consent forms and nod convincingly as her doctors explained the day's setback?

After "mom days" I crawl back to Eighty-eighth and Normandie tired but trying. The house buoys me before setting me off to sea again. Then there are the "nice fruit salad" days when Frances tells me to look for her AARP card in "the Afrocentric purse" and that I should paint the room we're all waiting for her to come home to a shade of green that's not "green green." Because she made me, I understand her completely. Those are the days I (we) get to fall into our old rhythm despite the awkward buzzing of the vital-signs machine that's throwing everything off beat.

But too often those daughter days had shrunk down to mere hours, spilling into the mom days, like the time Frances was "with it but fuzzy" and demanded that I eavesdrop on an "important conversation about alternative medicine" that, according to her, another patient was having in the room next door with veteran news anchor Connie Chung.

"I'm not going to do that, okay?" I told her in my practiced motherly daughter voice—it's forceful without being snippy.

"Go be a reporter!" Frances shot back.

"Yeah, no. That's what I'm not going to do." She rolled her eyes. I stared. She let it go only after I promised to look into it when I got home. I didn't.

Not too long after that, she calmed down enough to let me brush her hair—a tangled afterthought after the trauma we'd been through. I parted it down the middle, and as I worked each thick section into strong French braids running down either side of her head, my mother laughed, remembering a similar style her mother used to give her: "I called them my bullhorns." That was a good "mom day."

What's funny (besides the Connie Chung thing) about the question of motherhood and daughterhood is how easily the once permanent-seeming titles get wiped away. As a child I thought the parts we played were chiseled in stone; now it's as if they were scribbled hastily on a dry-erase board. They get wiped clean, then overwritten, and back again.

When I am my mother's mother, I get a glimpse of what she might have gone through raising me—the frustration, the unexpected reservoir of patience, the devotion—which in turn reminds me of the woman I want her to get back to. When I am her daughter, the sharp fear of losing her springs me into frantic action. And then I'm her mother again.

When my grandmother died, Frances found me at the wake worrying the inside of my lip in a back pew and "cheered me up" by wailing on my shoulder. I had wanted a good wallow on my own, but the Andrews women were nothing if not in solidarity when it came to screaming.

Ignoring my "I'm okay"s, my mother grabbed my hand and flipped it right and then left, inspecting the lifelines on one side and the wrinkles on the other. "It's okay," I said, knowing it wasn't but not knowing what else to offer the space between us. She cried harder, swallowing up the burst of grief that had flowed out of me just moments before.

"She'll never get to meet my granddaughter," my mother blubbered. I'd been married all of four months and grandkids were the last thing on my mind, but clearly the first on hers.

"Why are you even thinking about that right now?" I spat, immediately regretting my tone. She didn't say. She just kept crying and staring at my hands like a fortune-teller.

What does your mother become when you're becoming one yourself? What do you take and what do you leave? How many of her looks become yours? How many of her truisms get thrown in the trash? Where does she end and you begin? My mother got stuck somewhere between center stage and waiting in the wings. Taking up mental space that should've been the baby's.

Once Frances got out of the hospital, it was obvious to Rob and me, newly married and puffed up on our own futures, that we weren't out of the woods. One day we'd have to take care of my mother "for real." The uncertainty, the recklessness, the necrotizing fasciitis. "The Frances situation" was never-ending. This was a woman who never met a place she didn't eventually want to move away from. Never met a doctor whose advice she wouldn't ignore. She was free but also unmoored. We had to be her anchor, a ten-ton fact that imbued me with a renewed sense of responsibility—and, simmering on the back burner, deep, deep rage. Frances left the hospital after nearly four months on the inside. That was spring. By the summer I was pregnant. Shit was really getting real.

According to a 2012 Pew Research study of "the sandwich generation," "Nearly half (47%) of adults in their 40s and 50s have a parent age 65 or older and are either raising a young child or financially supporting a grown child. . . . And about one-in-seven middle-aged adults (15%) is providing financial support to both an aging parent and a child." "Sandwich" is a nice image. Sandwiches are delicious. Sandwiches save time. A particularly delicious one delivered at precisely the right moment might save a marriage. What this generation was experiencing was more like being caught in a medieval torture vise. Crushed.

In our Land of Make Believe, Frances, with her new lease on life, could live with us while helping take care of the baby, like how they do in every other country but America. It would be the whole "it takes a village" proverb IRL. A win-win. With these rose-colored goggles on, we dove into the deep end completely oblivious to how sharp Baby Shark's teeth really are.

Plenty of honest women will warn you about how much you'll

hate your husband after having his baby. He will drive you mad with his seeming inability to do anything besides ask dumb questions like "Where are the wipes?" and "Can she eat yogurt?" and "Are these the socks you want her to put on?" It's a stereotypical patriarchic trope that twenty-first-century cisgender couples should have moved past in favor of equitable child-rearing or whatever. We haven't, though. And I have never wanted to murder another human being more. Then my mom moved in.

The plan was for Frances to help us with Sally and for Sally to bond with her sole living grandmother, an heirloom chain we didn't want to break. Also, we could never in our wildest dreams afford daycare, so, *Welcome home, Mother, please don't drive me to Xanax.* I should've had that last bit tattooed across her surgical scar, because drive me fucking bonkers she did.

Only Christ himself knows whether it was the raging hormones, my own righteous female anger, or Frances's allergy to doing dishes, but in no time it became abundantly clear that my mother was not a squishy grandma throwback made up of Werther's Originals and warm hugs. Every time I had to wash an errant bowl of week-old baby food left to fester in a forgotten corner or remind Frances once again to stop inviting random strangers into our home to cornrow her hair, I silently seethed: *How the hell did you raise a kid? How am I even alive right now? Am I alive right now?* She was a shitty roommate and sometime babysitter all wrapped up in this musty rainbow muumuu she insisted Sally loved.

Unsurprisingly, given my hatred of confrontation, the three of us danced around like this for nearly six months before our first major blowup. Rob was working late; I was hangry after surviving the day on only a sad desk salad; and Frances had been on Sally duty. I got as far as our entryway before a tiny ball of human was thrust in my face. "She probably needs her butt butt changed," my mother offered before disappearing to her lair, also known as our "finished" basement. Sally was not with the shits and spent the next hour and a half shrieking as I tried to send after-hours emails, feed her milk my breasts made, bathe her squirming body without secondary-drowning her, read to her like the books said, and get her to sleep with enough time for me to guzzle a glass of wine before my own bedtime. She. Would. Not. Stop. Crying. I was tightrope-walking on my last nerve, and my daughter was not impressed by my athleticism. This baby wanted to speak to whoever was in charge! She dialed the volume up to earsplitting, and something in me cracked.

Throwing my head back, I howled my frustration at the ceiling, "Ahhhhhhhhhh!" That felt good. I did it again, and again, and one last time for good measure, screaming along with the baby, because when in Rome. When I checked my sanity in the mirror, just who do you think was staring back me? Frances, y'all. It was Frances. She appeared silently, wafting near the nursery doorway like the Ghost of Woodstock Past, complete with a floating, wild, gray Afro and that goddamned muumuu.

"Jesus Fucking Christ!" I barked. "You scared the shit out me." Did I mention Sally was still wailing at the top of her lungs? The noise was next-level. Then Frances did something I will never ever forget.

Inexplicably, my mother started singing.

"Laaaaaaaaaah," she chanted, adding her soprano to our sad symphony. Because no, Sally still hadn't stopped crying, and my mother thought, what? That her siren song would cancel everything out? That my eardrums needed a good beating? Either way, I was piiiiissed.

So I screamed some more, because everybody else was doing it. If a benevolent alien had been peeking through our window at that precise moment in order to determine whether the human race could join some intergalactic utopia, we'd be doomed.

I was mad at Frances for being so unhelpful and then suddenly so terrifyingly helpful. Mad at her for getting so sick in the hospital the year before that she now walked with the deliberate soft-shoe of the decrepit. Mad that she was old. Mad that her showing up out of nowhere put a pit of fear in my stomach that reminded me of the ICU and all we'd been through. Mad we still weren't over it. Mad that despite pouring every ounce of energy I could muster past 6 P.M. into calming Sally down, this baby still would not shut up. Mad. Mad. Mad.

"Why do you keep creeping up the fucking stairs? Do you think sneaking up on me is helpful?"

"I-I-I-I wasn't trying to sneak up on you," Frances stuttered, her voice cracking between pitiful and angry. "D-d-don't accuse me of doing things I didn't do!"

My eyes grew wide as saucers. Was she really trying to make this about her? "Out!" I shouted (yep, now we were all crying), pointing to the door behind her. "You need to get out of here."

My mother froze, a deer in the blazing headlights of my repressed rage. Things—and by *things* I mean my ability to control my volume and my vitriol—went downhill from there. We erupted against one another for what felt like forever. Me complaining about her inability to rinse out a bowl of baby cereal, and her, tears mixed with snot, wondering at my dumb luck. "At least you have a husband! I never had that." It was . . . a lot. And it wouldn't be our last fight over the six months that followed.

During the year she lived in my house—and cared for my daughter—the two of us toggled between versions of ourselves both new and old. We were the mother and daughter who spent eighteen years clinging to one another like life rafts. We were the mother and daughter who spent the next eighteen years thousands of miles from one another, clinging instead to memories. The mother and daughter whose lives the hospital surgically rearranged.

And now the mother and daughter who couldn't fit the pieces back together again.

It shocked me how quickly it happened. How Frances went from the Manic Pixie Dream Mom to the target subject of my group-chat rants. This woman had been my feminist hero, but after having Sally, all I could see were the gaping *no*'s in Frances's life. No partner. No house. No savings account. No plans beyond the next hare-brained scheme. At sixtysomething? The paradox of idolizing someone to the point of deification and then living long enough to lose your religion was soul-crushing in its way. How could she do this to me? To me. How could her life choices so irrevocably have influenced mine for all this time without me realizing? The free spirit I'd looked up to as a child—the woman whom I'd wanted nothing more than to be exactly like—now seemed so fragile and alone. That change was like a quake. I knew we would never be the same. And that admission felt like heartbreak. Or worse, a betrayal. But it shoved me hard into a new stage of adulthood. It's part of the reason I approached motherhood and babyhood and our neighborhood with such "know all the things" gusto. I didn't just want to be prepared. I wanted to be bulletproof.

CHAPTER **8**

Those Fucking Girls

"I seriously can't believe you hang out with those fucking girls," teased Sofia. "Like, how can you even stand them?" Yes, yes, I *know.* We sound like thirteen-year-old queen bees ragging on brainy mathletes (do folks even do that outside of early aughts teen rom-coms?) or, better yet, early-thirties worker bees griping about another "fun" Zoom happy hour. But no, we're old-ass women who know better than to trash-talk the latest clique (there's *always* a clique) tailor-made to make us feel both welcomed and worn out: the Mamas. Really, Sof is doing the trash-talking while I'm doing the *ummhmm*-ing, because little does she know that these chicks have succeeded in colonizing my time line.

To her, and all my "real" friends, the Mamas et al. represent an amalgam of every stereotypical Valley Girl villain. They can't help but picture them as the former sorority girls who stopped grinding on each other long enough to find mildly attractive husbands in law school, buy million-dollar flips, have the requisite 1.5 kids, and then kick-start a "mom group" for a growing cabal of parents

Columbusing the hidden-gem neighborhood they just discovered. It's the same way I saw them at first. As a gigantic blond mass rolling through the neighborhood like the blob. But it me! I'm sorta kinda one of them now, despite Sof's clowning to the contrary, which I wanted to dig into. Because in the age of Karens, and pussy hats, and protest signs that read DON'T FORGET WHITE WOMEN VOTED FOR TRUMP, the space between us and them seems to be growing rather than shrinking even while the other *everything*s (accountability, Covid, Kamala, the criminal cost of childcare) were allegedly bringing us together.

"I went to maybe one of those meetups when Lucy was born," explained Sof, who decided to have a baby on her own because "Why the fuck not?" and name her Luciana Serafina for the same reason. "It was ridiculous," she went on. "I didn't last five minutes. I just went to Target every day instead." She happily chose wandering aimlessly through discount Disneyland with a screaming baby over spending an afternoon a week tipping back nitro cold brews with the Plastic Moms of her own fancy neighborhood. I mean, I got it.

Andrea O'Reilly, the motherhood scholar, gets it too. Sprouting up mostly in urban centers, since those spaces are the most devoid of family support, mommy groups can be the surest path to a parenting community. But, added O'Reilly, they can also be, well, wack. "You can't always find your kind in those spaces," she said. "It's tough.

"They have the totally earned reputation of being performative, competitive, and judgmental. They aren't a place to let your hair down and complain about the kids and say you're having a shit day." These days they are also laser-focused on the children and not the overworked mommy. "There's not much time to talk during story time," said O'Reilly. And with this relatively new baby-centered focus, the modern mom group—which your average 1960s housewife might have called cocktails and a Valium with the girls—became very "homogenous and white."

"Other mothers—Black, younger, working class—often don't find them to be safe or nurturing spaces, so they opt out," explained O'Reilly. When she put that internalized exclusion into words, I couldn't help but nod. Opting out. It's the same reason I had completely sworn off a popular breastfeeding support group that was regularly recommended by the Mamas. My pal Monica (the one who wrote the tactful post about conflating class and race) wasn't so lucky. She went to "exactly one meeting" and threw the whole concept in the trash afterward. During her short stint, the mothers were discussing soothing techniques, essentially how to get your newborn to STFU, and the only other Black mom there besides my friend expressed concern about constantly picking up the baby. I already knew where this story was going before Monica finished.

"She was basically saying she didn't want to spoil the child by rocking it all damn day. You know, she needed to do other stuff with her hands, like take care of her older son who had special needs," recalled Monica, "and this little white girl got her panties all in a bunch. 'You can never spoil a baby! It's impossible. There's no such thing!' And I watched that woman curl into herself. God," she sighed, "it made me so mad." Monica never went back, and she doubts the other mother did either. This is what happens, according to O'Reilly and my own informal focus groups. Black moms show up to white-mom spaces and almost immediately do a turnabout, wondering what they were thinking in the first place. That's what makes us seek out one another instead, because we have something in common like Bobby and Whitney. But do we always?

Monica's story made me think about the advice my older cousin

LaDonna, who raised four boys on her own, gave me when I face-timed her with a two-month-old Sally drooling on my chest in an expertly assembled K'tan.

"You gonna spoil that baby!" she warned.

"You can't spoil a baby, crazy," I shot back, rolling my eyes.

"Ummmhmmm," said LaDonna through pursed lips.

We family, though. *We* can do that. We have a shared language, the same history, a deep understanding of one another's struggles and strengths that makes her "advice" ("sprinkle some browned flour on her butt, clear that diaper rash right up") both love and war. But that is us, it is not them.

So perhaps Sof was right. Those fucking girls and I could never truly get each other. Someone would inevitably make me run for the door. She didn't know them like I did, though. She didn't know who was battling infertility. Who was powering through the anniversary of their father's death. Whose parents had almost ruined their credit. Whose job had all but forced them out after they'd had the baby. Whose basement had flooded. Who needed a coffee break without a baby in tow before their head exploded. Walls separating us had been coming down for years but, as Sofia and Monica and Andrea and everybody pointed out, there was still a shadow over the whole thing. There always would be. I was getting used to that fact when the potential solution to my mom-friend conundrum presented herself suddenly. This was when Sally was super new and before Monica and I met. I was in the desert and there was the mirage. You guys, I spotted another bougie-looking Black woman with a baby in our hood.

Please don't be a nanny. Please don't be a nanny. Please don't be a nanny.

Our eyes locked as our mini ships approached each other on the sidewalk. She seemed as surprised to see me as I was to see her, slowing to a stop while I managed a covert glance into her Uppababy.

The plump toddler inside was a soft taupe to her glossy brown. Sooooo. Possible nanny? "Hiiiii," we both sang in that silly soprano women use to disarm each other. Nannies don't stop to say "Hi." A head nod and a smile are usually all they have time for. These women are working, not out making friends with the highfalutin ladies writing their checks. This was no nanny. I'd soon learn Tess— her name was Tess—was a first-timer like me. But unlike me, she had on flawlessly blended foundation at 1 P.M. and had two "properties in the area." Her disturbingly beautiful racially ambiguous baby looked like he had followers. He swept long bangs out of his impossibly big ole eyes while fiddling with a nontoxic toy. They were perfect. Eerily so. Before we went our separate ways, Tess offered up her info along with this tidbit: "There aren't too many of us." Then she pushed off in the opposite direction.

Almost every day afterward, my mother, who was living with us by then, asked if I had "connected with that lovely young woman we met on the sidewalk." My answer was always the same: "Not yet." And probably not ever. Truth is, I was terrified of Tess, which is funny because I spent my twenties dreaming about being her. Picturing myself someday slipping into Tess's perfect Olivia Pope wool coat is what got me through my crappy news assistant job and over another dumb boy who just wasn't "ready yet." *Someday.* Someday I would be that polished, that put together, that complete. I was sure of it. Then someday happened—marriage, momming, "mid-career." Was I one of those girls like Tess? I wasn't sure. And I wasn't alone. All my day ones were on the precipice too. Black professional women whose identities were stretching as we moved to different parts of the city and the country, digging into the lives we'd drunkenly mapped out over so many brunches.

My girl Gwen was seriously on track to run for office eventually, but then got married and had a kid and decided to cool it. We were sweating in a steam room when she told me how irate she got the day her husband gently prodded her about a potential promotion: "I couldn't do that job in a million years. Like how the fuck does he think all this other shit gets done?" Another friend, Camille, is currently trying to convince her seventy-five-year-old mother, who's been contemplating a divorce for, like, ever, not to build a tiny house in Camille's backyard. "Someone save me," she texted the other day after her mom presented her with some very expensive blueprints. Sofia relocated to San Francisco to live a block away from her lovable but certifiable parents. When that didn't work out, she moved two hours away. Of course, they decided to "surprise" Sof on the very day her new house was a hot mess (Sof had the flu, and her daughter, Lucy, was being a maniac). "This place looks like shit," her mother added helpfully. When Sofia broke down, launching into how hard it had been doing it all on her own, her mom hissed back, "Well, no one told you to do this." Actually, no one told us anything. Checked boxes didn't come with warning signs. Did we even want to be the women we were well on our way to becoming, or were we too busy to think of anything else? The answer was Tess.

I ran into her everywhere. Tess and her oddly grown-up handsome toddler with one of those last-name first names. At the park she told me about her son's first birthday: "We did pancakes and PJs! I hired a guy to sing nursery rhymes in French. I drank Bellinis alllll day." Another time she stopped me on the sidewalk and asked how I felt about public school.

"Uhhh. For?" I ventured.

"Me too!" she said. "I'm thinking about hiring a consultant to give a lecture about it at our house. Can you come?" Our kids were still in diapers. Was that going to be me in a year? Did I *want* that to be me in a year? I'd already been a fixture at classes and playdates and meetups, participating in all the intensive mothering there was on offer. But somehow following Tess down the rabbit hole seemed precipitous, perhaps even permanent.

I was one "We hired an au pair!" announcement away from going full Washington, becoming the kind of stroller-wielding, business-card-flinging, gentrifying thirtysomething Aaron Sorkin dramas are made of. It didn't take nearly as long as the alarmist headlines (BLACK WOMEN WILL DIE ALONE!) said it would to zoom from single, starving writer to *Washington Post* columnist taking care of an aging parent, an ambitious husband, and a drooling daughter. Wasn't Tess the template?

In the conclusion of their book *Big Friendship,* besties and podcast co-hosts Aminatou Sow and Ann Friedman talk about the various versions of a person that exist within a friendship. How friendship forces us to confront ourselves unfiltered. "Once you've seen yourself in a mirror of friendship—in both positive and challenging ways—the reflection cannot be unseen," they write.

We are constantly evolving and becoming—as our patron saint, Michelle Obama, would say. As our identities shift, so do our friendships (big, medium, and small). As we seek out others, who we're really looking for is ourselves. Sofia shamed me so much for joining the Mamas that I almost forgot that this was the same woman who'd taken Ubers to her daughter's daycare for a week because she found a dead horsefly in the backseat of her Beemer, refusing to drive it until "the situation was handled by professionals." Were we the same kind of mom? Andrea O'Reilly told me that finding your "kind" is a difficult task in the mom jungle, mainly because of separations in race and class, but also—and this is really important—because being a mom isn't a fixed identity.

We all come at this momming thing from different angles. Take me a Sof. Her parents have been attached at the hip for five decades; my mom's a rudderless bon vivant who once married a gay African friend because he needed a green card and she had nothing better to do. Yeah, that didn't last, her being a lesbian and all. But she had a story for her someday memoirs and I had the twenty-person white porcelain tea set he sent me one Christmas. Sof doesn't have student loans and I'm still hoarding a stack of past-due letters in my panty drawer. Her kid wears designer onesies and mine . . . are somewhere naked. Her daughter has more passport stamps than I do. But somehow, as moms of color raising babies of color, we're automatically the same, no matter what we look like on paper or whether we serve dinner on paper plates (raises hand). Society lumps us together, and when it comes to the challenges our kids as opposed to theirs face, I'm here for it. We're fighting the same fight in the principal's office and on the playground. But the woman has been trying for years to convince me to go on a luxury cruise with the kids while I'm like, why? The pattern might be the same but we're cut from a different cloth.

I didn't get that until my initiation into the larger world of the mom group, i.e., meeting a bunch of white moms, which blasted a gaping hole through every Pollyanna expectation I had about parenting just a few miles away from Barack and Michelle, whose own daughters went to an elite private school that cost the same as my college tuition. Are we the same? The Obamas and me, I mean. Man, I wanted us to be. But no, darling. Because in the end it didn't matter that I was an Ivy Leaguer, gainfully employed and legally saddled to my baby's father. Black was the first thing any other parent would see, whether they admitted it or not. And in all honesty, that's what I wanted. Being a Black mom *is* a particular calling with an undeniable history I am both immensely proud of and poised to combat. Yes, that was a lot of mental whiplash. If anything, being a Black parent has meant getting used to the roller coaster.

––––––––

Before I had Black children of my own to protect, I was protecting Black children. I don't like to talk about it much, mostly because of my natural inclination toward humility, but I'm a super badass, a heroine in plain sight. The year before I met Rob (and years before I ever imagined mixing our DNA), I did a bunch of crazy shit that I'm guessing was all divine preparation for what was to come. A test the universe was giving me to see if I could make the cut as a Black mom. First, I saved a nine-month-old from being sold into sexual slavery. Okay, fine, I called the police when I walked past a white man wildly swinging a baby in a car seat when it was 40 degrees out. A few months later I "saved" a teenage boy who'd been badly beaten by a pack of peers. Okay, fine, I called 911 and helped him out of the street. Not long after that I gave a group of horrible middle-school bullies, otherwise known as regular old tweenagers, a stern talking to in my best mom voice. That was a *Star Trek* moment, when the time line folded in on itself like an origami fortune-teller, and I got a peek into my past, my present, and my future.

I was out walking Miles when I passed an alley that seemed unusually packed with pubescent girls. I'm nosy and also terrified of zombies. So I stopped to investigate just in case the world was ending. Big Girl Energy was bursting from the brick—lots of shouting and jumping and *ohhhhhh*s, but no one was growling for fresh brains. I figured they were just girls being girls. School had just let out, and I remember well when the sound of the last bell was like a champagne bottle popping. They were the loud bubbles, clogging up the alley on their way out of the glass neck. Nothing more. I made a mental note of the mini mosh pit and kept walking. But a tingling on the back of my neck whispered for me to turn around seconds later. Call it curiosity, boredom (remember that before kids?), Jesus himself. I turned back just in time for the pony-tail parade. A group of girls spilled out onto the sidewalk, one excitedly waving a fist full of weave in the air and another shouting into a flip phone, "She's practically bald!"

None of that sounded like good clean fun to me.

When I crept silently (these girls were big, okay?) back to the mouth of the alley, I saw what they were so thrilled about. Two girls were going at each other against a garage door. One eventually knocked the other to the ground and proceeded to rain down kicks and punches like a cage fighter.

"Hey. Hey! *Hey!*" I shouted. The girl with the upper hand paused briefly to take in my black yoga pants and designer dog. She replied all too calmly, "Don't worry. It's okay," and then started again with the kicking and punching and the "Bitch this" and "Bitch that."

"No, *No!* It's *not okay!* Stop that. Right! Now! Go home." I've never shouted so furiously in my life, drawing from a well of mom voice buried deep. No one was listening, though. "*Go home!*" I yelled again.

Finally, they filed out of the alleyway, taking their sweet time gathering up the discarded machinery of their age littered about the sidewalk—JanSports, Mead notebooks, iPads. More than one of them called me an "old-ass bitch" and told me to "shut the fuck up" as I attempted to look authoritative and threatening in athleisure with my hand on my hip, my lips pursed, and my head cocked to one side. You've heard of the power stance. Well, that's the Black Mom stance. It was working until one of the girls decided to challenge me. To put it more plainly, she *danced* at me.

Like, I have no other way to describe it. This twelve-year-old literally planted herself a few feet in front of me, looked me straight in the eye, and proceeded to do coochie thrusts in her khaki uniform pants. This went on for three or four more thrusts as her friends laughed and I waited for the girl who'd been getting her ass kicked to escape in the opposite direction.

"Um, do you think you're cute?" I asked Ms. Coochie Thrust.

And then she seriously goes, "Nah." Thrust. "Do you?" Thrust. I'd give her thirteen, tops.

"No," I sighed, shaking my head. "I really don't. *Go home!*" It was surreal.

The whole debacle made me sad more than anything. Nothing says you're getting old more than a wannabe adult yelling, "Mind your business, bitch!" as she runs by, recording the whole thing on her phone. Someone brave has to say it: Teenagers are terrible people. Being the grown-up in the situation, I teetered between fear and being glad I was there, obviously to break up the fight, but also to point out to these girls that they are just that—girls.

I wrote about Ms. Coochie Thrust on a popular blog for women who wore pussy hats before they were a thing, and more than one commenter asked why I hadn't just called the police. A crime was committed. If that were my daughter, wouldn't I want her protected? Yeah, of course I would, which is why the thought of calling the police never crossed my mind. That's how white women think. Instead, I stood in the middle of the sidewalk blocking the fighters from the fought. I then quietly walked behind the girl who'd been hurt for an inappropriate amount of time for a stranger to be following a child home from school. I asked if she was okay more than once, and she responded with exactly one head nod. I was her shadow for a few blocks more. She never looked back.

In the years since, I've passed that same alley hundreds of times. It was on the way to work and later on the way to the daycare we chose for our daughters. When we stroll past on nice days, I can still hear those girls' shouts. Those fucking girls. How we rubbed one another raw until smooth.

I was on the way to meet some of the Mamas when Sofia sent me some child pornography. She got it from her daughter's preschool teacher. It featured a three-year-old Lucy, wide-eyed and all teeth, posing with her legs crossed like a grown woman and her otherwise completely appropriate ruffle-top dress pulled down past her shoulders like a vixen. The teacher thought it was cute.

"Okay, so just to be clear. This is because she's Black, right?" Sof asked with several angry-face emojis.

My response was swift. "Yes." "Absolutely." "Always." Because obviously, right?

There I was, strolling up to our tree at the park contemplating "adultification" of Black children as the moms of my neighborhood chatted happily about music class and moving out to the burbs. About how they chose a $2,500-a-month daycare because it was close to work, or a Haitian nanny because she spoke French. Meanwhile, I sat there bouncing a babbling Sally on my knee and thinking about how I would need to safeguard my daughter from being perceived as older and less innocent than she had every right to be. There'd even been a study released two months after Sally was born that basically proved that point. The Georgetown Law Center on Poverty and Inequality found that compared to white girls of the same age, Black girls were seen as needing less protection, less nurturing, and less support. Less. That our girls were perceived to be more independent and knowledgeable about adult topics, including sex. So, yeah, that picture of Lucy wasn't "cute." It was a snapshot of something symptomatic, how we as Black moms had to always be on the lookout for shit like that.

I couldn't show the group Sofia's text because they wouldn't get it. They couldn't. Plus—and maybe this is the real reason—I didn't want to be the Angry Black Mom, or worse, the Overreacting Black Mom. It was taxing. In those pre-pandemic, pre–George Floyd, pre-apocalyptic days, my time with those fucking girls, swaddled as they were in the privilege of not knowing, felt like a breath of fresh and rarefied air, all the crap of the outside world HEPA-filtered out.

I didn't want to stink it up with the reality of raising Black children in a code orange kind of world. Back then they were a welcome respite from "race stuff," which is to say the other twenty-three hours of my day. Of course, that vacation from reality was short-lived, but man, even the briefest of pauses can be a chance to breathe.

Forget partying like a white girl, what I really wanted, deep down in the sunken place, was to parent like one. All the love but minus the crippling legacy of institutionalized socioeconomic oppression and the baked-in fear that your child might get murdered while playing at the park. Heavy shit like that. And even though at the end of the day as an educated and employed Black woman I can sort of parent like a white girl (I mean, we had as much expensive baby "gear" as the next nuclear family), that's all just smoke and mirrors. Our stash was less about utility than it was evidence. See, we can do this too! Look at her many leather-bound books! But take away a paycheck or two, burn a few degrees, and we go from the Obamas on the cover of *Ebony* to the tragic Blacks of Trump's dystopian inner-city fantasy.

So we—Black professional educated parents—overcompensate, we course-correct. It's the reason I used to put on makeup to get on the Metro with the three-hundred-dollar stroller I described as "firmly midrange" when my mom asked why we were spending "so damn much." The reason I never left the house with the baby and without my wedding ring. Why every name we considered for our kids had to pass a test no one can study for. It's not so much keeping up with the Joneses as it is justifying our existence. Or at least that's what we're telling ourselves when the Amazon bill comes.

I think that's why in the beginning I spent so much time with the Mamas as opposed to with my Black friends with kids. I wasn't passing, I was moonlighting, if only temporarily, as a mom without worries.

To be clear, I worried with the best of them. All of us did. I worried about accidentally rolling over on my baby like that one chick in the Bible. And about those ants crawling into her ear at the park during the one millisecond I wasn't looking, my criminal negligence causing her to go deaf and also somehow blind. About not getting her into the "right" daycare. About not really caring if she was in a "dual language" anything at eighteen months. About crushing the poor kid with the weight of all my worrying. But the other stuff, the race stuff, that was a ton heavier, and it was always waiting there to be picked up and carried home after the blissfully ignorant coffees and strolls and baby yoga sessions.

The first time the topic of race finally did come up during a Mamas meetup, I was on high alert. We always are. Aminatou Sow and Ann Friedman, as interracial besties, dig into "the trapdoor" in *Big Friendship*. It's the feeling, first crystalized by culture critic Wesley Morris, that as the Black friend you have a ghost-limb awareness of the high probability that your white friend will say or do something racist. It's a matter of when, not if. And our proverbial booty cheeks are always clenched for the stomach-dropping plunge. For Aminatou and Ann, the trap wasn't quite so treacherous. They'd been close friends for years and trusted one another enough to work past any racial missteps. Not so for me and these fucking girls.

We were sitting on the lush grass of Crispus Attucks Park—you know, the one named after the Black man who was the Revolutionary War's first casualty—and discussing racial profiling, as you do. I don't remember how the topic came up, but I am sure I shared the story of how my husband was pulled over twice for "speeding" in a golf cart during our wedding weekend. Or the time our old neighbors called the cops on him for "walking around the building at night." To prove her street cred, one mom goes, "Oh yeah, like that Trayvon White." The look I gave her must have screamed, "What the fuck?" because I know I wanted to. "The kid? Who got shot? From Florida? Trayvon White?"

"Martin," I corrected. "Trayvon Martin." And I left it at that because I wasn't ready to be through with these women just yet. I didn't want to take my baby and go home, complaining to Rob once again about "the you know who's." I'd finally gotten into the swing of things, balancing the baby's constant needs with my new-mom mania, and I shared some of my emotional load with the Mamas, because they had room on their bare shoulders. The group was undoubtedly a balm—just so long as I didn't pick at the scab of race. After that first toe dip into the topic, I knew I couldn't "get into it" with these women, not yet or maybe not ever. My invisible hackles were up.

That's the thing about forming even the most tentative bonds with white women as Black women: We simply don't trust them. At least not at first, or maybe ever. Over centuries of mistreatment the suspicion has settled into our very bones.

Historian Katrina Moore, an associate professor at Saint Louis University, explained it this way: "Historically, Black women should not trust white women, like, period, until they prove themselves otherwise." Then Moore added, "And then you always have to watch." That's a Black woman's moral obligation—always watching. Like my neighbor Miss Joyce from her front porch, never letting up.

Often historians talk about "the split" between white women and Black women as allies happening somewhere around 1870 and the passage of the Fifteenth Amendment. Before that, white women were vocal and visible in the abolitionist movement, seemingly staunch supporters of the Black cause. But when Black men (and not white women) got the right to vote, white women bounced. That explanation is instructive but too simple, says Moore. The gap between Black and white women, she explains, was near insurmountable long before the late nineteenth century. Reaching back into the centuries of American slavery, enslaved Black women never found friendship with white women no matter what *Gone with the Wind* and *Uncle Tom's Cabin* had to say about it. Despite whatever shared gender oppression the two groups suffered as women, free white women were still light-years ahead of enslaved Black women in the social, economic, and political hierarchy. And white women relished that superiority.

"At the end of the day, you still want to be on top of a crab. We're all in the bucket, but you still want to be a little bit higher," said Moore in an interview. "So white women and Black women—even when there's a common cause, race is always that dividing factor. Once race was constructed, then the hierarchy was set. Therefore, friendships will always be questionable, alliances will always be questionable, because people have to get past the whole idea of what race is. That's a lot to get past."

So we, Black women, have learned to be on edge around white women. We've learned that as soon as their interests don't align with ours they'll turn on us. It's a parable that repeats itself from slavery all the way up to Trump's presidency. It's why Sofia couldn't get why I spent any amount of time with them. Why Monica never stepped foot in that breastfeeding group again. Why white commenters thought I should call the police on a group of Black children. Why Lena Hodge couldn't fathom having a Black neighbor. It's that cement wall none of us can see but all of us can feel the weight of.

"The story was written before any of us were born, before our grandmothers were born. Paranoia, once it set in, it stayed," said Moore. "Nothing has happened to tell us that we should not keep that. You have enslavement, Reconstruction; then the Klan starts, Jim Crow, the Civil Rights Movement, the crack epidemic, and this whole time police have always been shooting us. When should we have relaxed?"

The answer, obviously, is never. Not at the voting booth or on a picnic blanket in the park trading diaper blowout war stories. It's another reason Sofia's warning about "those fucking girls" sounded like an alarm. The past—lived, learned, and ignored—could be an insurmountable obstacle.

Denene Millner, the author and publisher, put it plainly. "I just understand with fifty-two years under my belt that the push on their part to understand and be better is fragile. It's there for the moment, but the second it feels uncomfortable? They're done. I refuse to be surprised by it or be hurt by that. You really have a hard rock to crack to get me to a place where I trust you."

When I think of the impact of racism in America, I think of *Star Trek*. Stay with me. One of the mainstays of the sci-fi series is the space-time continuum, which asserts that time itself isn't a linear thing to be experienced from point A to point B in chronological order. Instead, it can be kneaded like dough, folded onto itself and smashed together. White people perceive race and racism as spilled milk, annoyingly sticky for a time but eventually swiffered off the kitchen floor, never to be thought of again—or at least not until more milk is spilled. But I'm dough. No, I was never enslaved, was never sterilized against my will, spat on at a lunch counter, or sued for buying a home on a white street. But, see, I was. It's in my guts, constantly simmering in my insides.

Now imagine bringing *that* up when the group is sorting out the benefits of one nursing bra over the other. Laying my deepest fears bare for consumption. That's the other thing that will get in the way of an interracial friendship—vulnerability. Could I ever feel like my complete self among these women? That was a question novelist Deesha Philyaw had when she was raising her first child in suburban Pittsburgh among mostly white women. The answer was no. She never felt truly herself. "I was playing a role as a wife and a mother. It felt like a performance," she told me during a candid conversation about what it means to be a Black mother figuring her own self out.

It didn't help that the trapdoor opened during one of Philyaw's mom meetups. "Finally, one of them said the thing I was dreading, 'I always wanted to have a Black friend.' Ah! Why did you have to go and say it?" recalled Philyaw.

Nothing overtly racist happened while Philyaw did her time as a religious, married, stay-at-home mom of the Pittsburgh burbs, she just never felt truly at ease in that setting, like a fly in buttermilk, as my great-grandmother would have said. "With white women it always felt like a project. It always felt like work. I never felt like 'Ohhh, I really want to hang out with her.' All the moms were just together by matter of fact," she said. Eventually Philyaw moved to the city, got divorced, and started hanging out with kidless artists and moms who did quirky shit like run printing presses out of their garages. These were her people. The shift was seismic and Philyaw left her version of "those fucking girls" in the dust. "When I tell you I just stopped talking to those suburban white women. I mean, talk about ghosting. I ghosted everybody. I don't miss them. It was like a reinvention."

For Philyaw it wasn't just about race, it was about compatibility. White or not, those moms just weren't her tribe. And once she found one of her own, it was a wrap. I, on the other hand, was wrapped up in these streets, this neighborhood, and its emerging identity. The mom group was an indelible part of that stew; bowing out felt like giving them more hard-won ground. We're not escaping to a bohemian dreamscape with 99 percent Black people, no fireworks after 9 P.M., and a 100 percent walkability score. Believe me, I looked. Instead, we're staying put. As Miss Connie says, "The neighborhood needs you." The commitment to it is a resistance in ways both real and imagined. The history here, the community, the short walk to work. It is ours, and I have the Ring cam footage to prove it. Putting down roots meant more than just putting up with the parents around here. I didn't want to simply tolerate them or walk on a tightrope around them. Ducking into Target like Sofia for hours at a time to avoid the inevitable wasn't an option. That meant dealing with those fucking girls.

Oddly enough, the person I never had to deal with again was Tess. The years went by. We had another baby girl, saved for a house we probably still couldn't afford; Sally started school, and I never saw Tess again. I even texted her once to see if she wanted to join me and some other Black moms at the local library to chat about school choice. The very thing Tess had cornered me about a few years before. She never texted back. It was weird. Did I have the right number? The right mind? Had I imagined her appearing out of the fog of new motherhood just when I needed a Black face to pin my fears to like some kind of *Sixth Sense* situation? Because what's really eerie is that just as Tess ghosted me the neighborhood suddenly became overrun with Black moms. Okay, "overrun" is a bit much. There were like six of us. But still! We had a quorum.

Monica was "living the Cosby dream" in a big-ass Victorian a few blocks from our struggling front porch. I first ran into Lynne on the corner with her daughter strapped to her chest and immediately ran down all the Bloomingdale mom shit there was on offer. "Just give me your email address," I told her. Now she's the emergency contact on my daughter's school forms. After nearly a decade living abroad, my college friend Denise, an international banker, was back with a wife and a daughter. The happy trio moved into a three-bedroom that was a three-minute stroller ride away from our house. Amber lived with her husband and two kids in the house her grandparents had fought for. Slowly but surely, we had a squad, and realizing that there weren't "many of us," the unspoken rule was that we'd stick together. We even met up regularly at Crispus

Attucks Park to infiltrate, letting our brown babies and big kids run around like they owned the place, because they did, too. At one such takeover we watched in awe from picnic blankets as the children hunted for Easter eggs and chased butterflies. An easy scene that meant double to us, one Tess would've approved. A scene the Mamas would always take for granted.

Was *this* my authentic self? Or, like Deesha, my reinvention?

Thing was, I still hung tight with "those fucking girls" too, still chastised all my Black mom friends who weren't in "the Facebook group," because we all had to be in the know. We had to be paying attention. Plus, guys, those girls weren't all bad! I swear. Take Meghan, who lived on the same block as my friend Chioma, a D.C. native whose parents initially gave their only daughter's historic Bloomingdale row house the side-eye. "They thought the neighborhood was dangerous," she explained, because during their heyday it was. Chi worked in public policy, like Meghan, and when I described "my friend" who lived two houses away, Chi's face screwed all up. "Oh, her?" she said. "She never speaks."

CHAPTER **9**

That Other *Talk*

Black daughters felt like dodging a bullet. Before Sally and Robyn, I had been terrified of birthing a Black son. Of fiercely loving a Black boy. Of being rewarded for that bottomless love with a hole. Of having to watch his back as it walked out of my front door. Of having "the talk" with him and hating myself for it.

Whether you're woke or hitting the snooze button under a post-racial rock, you've heard of "the talk." It's the sit-down we have with our children—usually preteen sons—about how to contort and comport themselves around the police. "The talk" is both a necessary survival tactic and a macabre rite of passage, meant to protect our boys from the immediate physical dangers of racism while welcoming them into Black manhood before any child should begin packing away their childish things. *Sure, you still sleep on PJ Masks sheets, but it's past noon on your boyhood, and these racist adults are waiting patiently outside. Mazel tov!* During "the talk," which is separate but equal to the birds and the bees, traditionally fathers instruct their sons on what to do with their bodies. Don't look threatening, do smile, don't show teeth, do look them in the eyes, don't look them in the eyes, do put your hands up, don't reach for anything, and never ever turn your back on them.

It's your duty as a Black parent to deliver it. It's not an option; it's an obligation. Passed down from generation to generation for centuries, the talk has no script but can be recited by most. It's a fact of Black life that white people have "discovered" in recent years. It has its own Wikipedia page. A dedicated entry on WebMD. And I thought that having a girl was equal to a hall pass—or at least a "let me tell you all about racism" rain check. I'd spent many pregnant weeks toggling between the extremes of joy and fear—excited about the baby and terrified that the two of us might not make it out of the hospital together. Since, according to all the devastatingly accurate doomsday headlines and expert research, Black women are three to four times more likely to die in childbirth than white women. Simply surviving seemed like a triumph. Add a boy to the mix and the laundry list of dangers didn't stop there. He couldn't safely play at the park, buy something from a store, walk home after, jog, drive, breathe. A girl would be a welcome breeze.

I know, I know. The sense of relief was like sand through my fingers. Black women have had it every way but easy in America. But for that painfully brief moment in the doctor's office, the idea of a girl child was a balloon. Then, of course, she landed earth-side and I had to share her with the rest of the world, i.e., those fucking girls. Girls (and boys, but come on, it *always* starts with girls) who, from the time they can talk and walk, possess the power to rip apart the concrete confidence I've been pouring into my daughters since before I knew them. Tiny wolves, dressed in little girls' clothing, who I recognized from my own childhood (and from college and the office and the marches). Girls whose otherwise typical mean-girl-in-training behavior wouldn't grate so much if it weren't directed at the *only* Black girl. Girls I tried to keep Sally away from but who were unavoidable in a neighborhood, nay a country, like ours. So cue that *other* talk. The one I didn't see coming until it was already giving me some serious stank eye from a pink Schwinn.

This is the story of why I told off a six-year-old—and would do that shit again.

Let's start with Sally. To truly understand my firstborn and why I—an adult on paper—would get into it with a kindergartener on her behalf, we must blame her father. She's his mini-me in more ways than one. Much like Rob, Sally has never once met a stranger. All unknown members of the animal kingdom are friends-in-waiting, folks who don't know how much they missed Sally's high-pitched "*Hi!*" until they hear it for the first time. Without filter or fear, she bum-rushes new "best friends" within seconds of meeting them. It's all cute until my baby gets stiff-armed by a six-year-old who's reached her buddy limit for the day. Sally, though, is rarely deterred by something as intangible as boundaries. "Go away!" is an invitation to smile wider, laugh louder—to show this *other* little girl what she's missing. God, it's delightful and painful to watch from a park bench. Clocking my child trying to convince random kids she's cool. I usually let these abbreviated morality plays run their course—the kid in question eventually gives up and in. Except when the object of Sally's unrequited affections is white. For reasons both personal and problematic, I cannot stand it when my daughter chases after little white girls at the park who want nothing to do with her. My Black Mama hackles rise, and I go into attack mode.

On the afternoon in question, I'd had enough. Sally was running behind a little asshole dressed in an Elsa costume. Okay, okay, *asshole* is harsh. The girl was fine, I guess. She had a flat curtain of auburn hair cut in a sharp edge along her shoulders and all the assuredness of a kid wearing glittery high-tops, polka-dot leggings, and a well-loved princess dress. Sally, a *Frozen*-head, was smitten. From my perch at a bench not far away I watched nervously as my daughter did what she does.

"Hi! My name's Sally," she huffed cheerily while running alongside this little girl who was so clearly ignoring her. Undeterred, Sally kept at it, following this silent child from swing to slide, and trying her damnedest to get her attention. "Do you like Olaf? I like Olaf!" The girl stared through my child as if she didn't exist—and maybe to her she didn't. There was clear evidence of Little Elsa's ability to laugh and play. She'd been doing plenty of both with another kid when we arrived. But add Sally to the mix and now the recipe for good old-fashioned fun was somehow ruined. She looked at my daughter, my radiant child, as if she were radioactive, immediately running in the opposite direction whenever Sally got close. It goes without saying that to my big-girl eyes (and baggage) Sally's skin was the kryptonite. There are other Black kids besides mine in our neighborhood (I know because we've conscripted nearly every one of them), but unless we intentionally roll deep to the playground, they're almost always outnumbered. It wouldn't be shocking for Elsa to not have any real Black friends. For her to see my daughter as an unknown, a non-factor, a problem to be ignored. Before Sally can launch into her smooth-jazz rendition of "Let It Go" and things really go off the rails, I step in.

"Sally. Sally. Come here, butter bean," I call. She reluctantly trots over, annoyed that I'm interrupting her latest conquest with my idiosyncrasies.

"Mommy, my new friend has an Elsa costume. Elsa!"

"That's not your friend," I deliver bluntly, hoping not to sound too harsh, but Band-Aids need ripping. "That's just some girl in a dress. You *have* friends. Vivienne, Zora, Zola, Kai, Malcolm, Mackenzie, Winter, Sadie . . ." I rattle off every brown-skinned child Sally has ever known, reminding her she's got people.

"She *is* my friend!" Sally announces defiantly, before running in Elsa's direction once again. I back off but not away, squinting across the artificial turf for any sign of something not right. Sally repeatedly tries and fails to get Elsa's attention. Okay, this kid *is* an asshole. I'm sorry. She's gone from aggressively snubbing my child to baiting her, basking in Sally's attention then hopping on her pink bike and pedaling away just as Sally gets close. Finally, my baby girl is starting to get it, and goes to sulk by the swings with her head hanging low. Have you ever seen a child with the shoulders of defeat? Oh, it's a gut punch. I was on my way to deliver a pep talk when Elsa comes at me, bro. Like, she legit pulls up. Let me repeat: This six-year-old pedals full speed in my direction and stops short with a screeching halt and stares me down like she's tryna start some shit. *Oh, honey. We can do this if you want to.*

Hand on my hip, I dramatically cock my head to one side, "*Hello.*"

The child says nothing. She just keeps glaring at me like she's waiting for an apology. *Who is this kid?*

"Hel-looooo," I repeat a little louder. "It's polite to speak when spoken to. Didn't your mother teach you that?"

She mumbles something and I hit another meme-able move, rotating my stank face so that my ear can hear her. "Excuse me? What did you say?"

"Hi," she whispers in a tone that's more self-satisfied than shy, and she's still drilling holes with her eyes. Did I mention she was six, maybe five? I did. Okay. "I said 'Hi.'"

"Ummhmm," I grump through pursed lips my aunties would applaud. "It's *also* polite to greet new friends or at least let them know you'd like to play alone. But don't worry, Sally's good. She is *very* fun and we're going to have a great time on the swings. Good day!"

Then I jog over to my daughter, who is still moping, and commence to show her the time of her little life at that playground. We ran, we jumped, we laughed, we swung, we sang, we dug purposeless holes and then filled them with rocks. It was a time. And all the while I narrated each moment like a Greek chorus for an audience of one—Elsa.

Later, when I told Rob about the whole saga, he was mortified. "Please do not be that Black mom giving little kids the business at the playground. What if someone did that to Sally?"

"Uh, no. First off," I said, "no one would dare. Because, second, why would they? She's not an asshole. I had to let this little girl *and* Sally know!"

"Know what?" asked Rob.

Good question. What teachable moment was I trying to impart to my daughter and this four-foot tyrant? That Black is beautiful? That children are ready for Critical Race Theory? That I am ready to flip cars and kindergarteners should they pose a threat to mine? All of it.

"That our kid is fucking fantastic," I shout because really that was it. He shook his head and forbade me (*tuh!*) from going off on any more children not my own. Fine, Rob didn't get it. But when I told other moms of color about Racist Elsa—about how since that day I'd become hyperaware of Sally's every interaction with white kids—instead of wagging their fingers, they nodded their heads. Every last one had a near-identical story of their child being othered by otherwise innocent-looking little people in ways both *"Did I just hear that?"* subtle and *"Not today, Satan!"* overt. And every last one bent over backward to soften the blow.

"I mean, it's really hard to call a four-year-old racist," admitted one of my brown mom friends. But . . . if it walks like a Donald, right? I could still hear the anger and anguish in this woman's voice when she recalled an *"Is this what I think it is?"* scenario with her then three-year-old son. The mark (and mission) it left was still fresh. When her oldest started preschool—one of those liberal co-op deals that's catnip to progressive parents—there was one kid, a little white girl, who singled him out whenever she got the chance. Day in and day out, she excluded him from play and got the other kids in on the game too, ostracizing him at school. And yes, he was the only nonwhite kid there. "I don't think he knew what was happening or why," said this mother. "It still hurts, though," she added, remembering her own interactions with mean white girls in elementary school and her mother's response: "Those girls are just ignorant." My mom had an equally unhelpful refrain—the time-worn "sticks and stones." Words might not physically hurt, but man they could cause damage.

And that's more of the invisible load threatening to bring down this flight—our own baggage as former little Black and brown girls looking for love in all the white spaces. None of us came out unscathed, and in trying to save our children from the same scars we question whether we're helicoptering too close. Because, come on, all children can be irrational maniacs. Anyone who's spent an hour explaining to a snot-sobbing four-year-old that she can't wear those dirty-ass rain boots to school knows this. What was happening to my friend's son wasn't your average preschool foolishness, though. Any uncertainty (because remember, we often feel that creeping "Am I overreacting?" self-doubt) about the true source of this little girl's wrath was squashed when a Black boy was added to the fray. She immediately switched her focus and started shitting on him, the darker brother. "I hated this little girl so much," confessed my friend with a laugh that tried to cover up the guilt you inevitably feel as a grown-up fantasizing about thrashing a little kid. But it's not just in our imagination.

There are reams of research pages dedicated to racial preference among children. Babies as young as three months can spot physical differences and prefer the faces of certain racial groups, i.e., the

folks they know. Duh. As they begin to make sense of their expanding world, older and more mobile babies use race to categorize,
grouping like with like. Again, completely logical. But as the
months and years pile up, so do the potential land mines. By three
years old, some kids start associating certain characteristics and
behaviors with certain racial groups. Ruh-roh! In the United States
a four-year-old has the mental capacity to associate white skin with
wealth. By kindergarten white kids in America demonstrate strong
"in-group" bias, meaning they prefer other white kids over everybody else. Black children the same age, however, don't show that
same level of racial preference. Surprised? I'm not. And yet when
the research comes roaring to life and statistics jump from the page
to the playground, it's still a shock to your system. Or as my friend
said when recalling how her son (how she) felt when that little
white girl acted exactly how the smarties studying this bullshit pre-
dicted she would, "It still hurts."

My good friend Lynne, yes that same Lynne who had no problem calling out misbehaving children (Black or polka-dotted), was
more than hurt when her daughter, Marley, breezed through the
back door after a morning spent at the park and delivered this blow:
"Mommy, G said he didn't like Black people."

"Helena," Lynne fumed, "I was ready to knock down every door
in this neighborhood." Filled to the brim with the righteous fury of
the Black Mama, Lynne, a woman so preternaturally nice I was
afraid to befriend her at first lest my own human awfulness come to
light, switched instantly to safety mode. First, she got to the bottom of it. What the hell had happened? According to her nanny
(yes, we have nannies too), Marley had been playing happily at
Crispus Attucks with another girl, who happened to be white. Then
this child's big brother showed up, we'll call him G, and he wanted
in on the fun the girls were having. But, using the illogic of tiny
humans, his little sister rebuffed him: "No boys allowed!" G's

response was swift: "Fine! I don't like Black people, anyway." Oh, and G's nanny, who watched the whole scene unfold, was Black. Child, it was a mess.

Thankfully Marley came home more confused than wounded. "She told me 'We didn't do anything to make him say that,'" recalled Lynne. Marley had dragged the little white girl into the boat with her, thinking "Black people" referred to the both of them. "That was a dagger in the heart," said Lynne, who had to switch hats once again, tabling her temper in favor of offering her daughter a soft landing. She delivered a sermon about how some people think they are better than others because of the color of their skin and that some parents teach their kids these horrible ideas. "Of course, we reinforced that her skin is beautiful and that it looks like Mommy and Daddy's skin." And before bed that night, mommy and daughter watched Oscar-winning actress and all-around goddess Lupita Nyong'o read from her book *Sulwe,* about a little girl with skin the color of a Night Cap calla lily and learning to love how perfect it was.

The next morning Marley woke up having already moved on, and Lynne was on her way to the park. She wasn't going to let G off the hook. Lynne and I have an unspoken rule when the girls are "the only ones" on the playground—we silently hand off watching their exchanges with *other* kids, like parents at the pool making sure their children don't drown. Lynne didn't see G that day or any day after, but made her nanny promise to say something if she ever saw him again. A week later she handed Lynne the following note written in G's ham-handed script:

Dear Marley,
I am very sorry for saying racist words
and hurting your feelings.
I will not do it again.

Lynne never showed Marley that note. Why would she? The child couldn't read and, more important, she didn't need the useless weight of other people's "racist words." Lynne folded it back up and put it in a drawer.

The hard truth about apologies is that they are never for the person being apologized to, not really. What does "I'm sorry" do for the bruise already forming? The water from your eyes nearly dry on your pillow? It brings you back to a pain that's on its way to mending, a memory best forgotten. Which isn't to say you shouldn't apologize to people. Just don't expect "people" to thank you for it.

This is how my friend Trina felt when the family of the little girl who'd introduced her daughter to racism wouldn't let up with the liberal outrage, the wanting to talk it out, the overexplaining—the apologizing, apologizing, apologizing. Their kid had done a thing. A thing that rocked Trina to her core and forever changed how she navigated the places she thought were safe. But Trina didn't want more apologies. She wanted that *other* girl and her family to deal with their own shit. While she cleaned up the mess on her end.

"This is the thing you have to know first," Trina explained to me. "My husband and I both grew up in predominantly white spaces." As a Black child raised in the Midwest, she'd been called the n-word, told she was dirty. "It was super important to us that she never experience what we experienced." Like so many Black parents with the means and privilege to cultivate their children's lives, Trina and her husband intentionally filled their baby girl's world with everything Black—friends, church, activities, doctors, everything.

But when the pandemic hit, she and her husband, both in demanding professional careers, placed their daughter in a "pod" with other kids at her otherwise very Black public school. The pod, which wasn't free or cheap, was the first time Trina's daughter was "the only one." They were uncomfortable from jump but also in an impossible position childcare-wise. So they sucked it up and hoped for the best. Less than a week in, Trina's daughter had a question: "Mommy," she asked so plainly that the slap that came next was a surprise, "are Black people bad?" Trina cries not a little remembering that night. Her voice is shaking.

"I know this is going to sound crazy, but we hadn't even told her she was Black," recalled Trina. The words necessary for "the talks" hadn't even entered her parenting lexicon yet. She, like many of us avoiding the inevitable, thought she had more time. But remember my *Star Trek* theory? Time is never just waiting. The past, the present, the future, are all right there.

In an article for *The Atlantic* titled "What's Lost When Black Children Are Socialized into a White World," journalist and author Dani McClain explored how families of different races broached the subject of race with their children. "Parents of color," wrote McClain, "are about three times as likely to discuss race with their children as are white parents, according to a 2007 study of kindergartners and their families in the *Journal of Marriage and Family*." The majority of white parents (three out of four) in that same study steered clear of the topic of race altogether. One reason for the discrepancy? White parents think talking about race in and of itself is racist, explained McClain, pointing to research published in the 2009 book *NurtureShock*. Instead of contextualizing race and racism in America for their kids, white parents went with a "See no evil" approach that emphasized color blindness despite all the evidence to the contrary. "When white parents leave kids to make sense of these contradictions on their own, without historical context or guidance on how to think about difference, classrooms are bound to become fraught spaces for black children," explained McClain, who is also the author of the book *We Live for the We: The Political Power of Black Motherhood*.

Trina knew all this, but in the bath that night with her daughter asking if Black people were bad, she felt caught off guard and completely unprepared. Actually, more than that, it was as if all the choices she'd made, her instincts as a Black Mama, weren't enough.

"Me and my husband, we literally tailored our whole life for her never to have to go through this. We live in a Black city. Send her to Black schools. I did all the things I was supposed to do. So we never sat her down. We didn't need to. She was constantly around little Black girls . . . I don't even know what's happening right now," explained Trina, her voice quaking. "And she's asking me so plainly. I mean, she's smiling. 'Are Black people bad?'"

And like all of us, Trina's first instinct was to get to the bottom of it. Where had this come from? What was happening? And like always, it came from one of those fucking girls. Since starting the pandemic pod Trina's daughter had made friends with another little girl we'll call K.

"K said Black people were bad," recalled Trina's daughter that night in the bath.

"Are you sure she said that?" Relating that response to me a year later, Trina is surprised her knee-jerk reaction was to question her own child, question what she'd heard. She just couldn't believe it. "I kept being like, maybe she misunderstood. Tell me everything. She had a whole story and it never changed." Trina's daughter and K had been looking out a window when they saw a Black man carrying a package down the street. "Black people are bad," K told Trina's kid. "And he probably stole that." Right.

Trina did what Black Mamas do. She went into clean-up mode, just like Lynne had with Marley and I had with Sally. She ticked off all the Black people her daughter knew. "We're Black. We're all nice people." She then gave her a prepared comeback, a speech to give in case K or anyone said some nonsense again, because of course they would. Later that night, after she put her daughter to bed, Trina immediately jumped on the phone, making sure the pod leader knew what had happened and that it could never happen again.

The grown-ups leapt into action. K's parents were notified and apparently mortified. The next morning Trina tried to play it cool; she didn't want her daughter to feel an ounce more discomfort, so she dropped her off hoping she remembered that speech from the night before and where she came from in general.

Ten minutes later Trina's phone rang. It was the pod leader, a Black woman. It had happened again. She had overheard Trina's daughter telling K, "Stop saying that. Black people are not bad. My mommy and daddy are nice." They sent K home. In between apologies and begging for the chance to explain themselves, K's horrified parents had one common refrain: "We don't know where she's getting this from!"

Sociologist Margaret Hagerman knows exactly where K and G and Racist Elsa get it from. Hint: their parents.

For two years, Hagerman studied more than two dozen upper-middle-class Midwestern white families, observing how parents and their children perceived race and racism. What she found out is compiled in the book *White Kids: Growing Up with Privilege in a Racially Divided America.* Hagerman's conclusion is simple: Kids don't do what we say; they do what we do. So instead of simply telling children that racism is, well, bad, parents need to walk the walk as well, living that tenet by consistently practicing antiracist behavior. Like, you know, having more than one Black friend—or maybe even one.

"White kids learn about race as a result of their own independent experiences—not just conversations," wrote Hagerman in *Time* magazine. "Their lived experience and their interactions with peers, teachers, neighbors, coaches, siblings and strangers matter greatly. The choices parents make about how to set up children's lives influence their kids' ideas about race and racism. The neighborhood they live in, the school they attend and the activities they participate in—sports leagues, religious organizations, clubs, summer camps—set the parameters for how kids understand race. And this is true whether parents are consciously aware that these choices matter or not, and regardless of what parents explicitly say about race."

Hagerman spent a mountain of mind-numbing hours with white preteens and teens to understand how they learned about race. As she watched them go about their daily lives—clowning around with friends, barreling through homework, playing video games—one thing became clear: You are who you hang around with. White kids immersed in diverse social, educational, and extracurricular circles were what a time traveler from 2016 would call "woke." One eleven-year-old in the "diverse" group informed Hagerman that racism "is a *way* bigger problem than people realize."

At the other end of the spectrum were the kids entrenched in predominantly white settings (their neighborhood, school, church, soccer team, etc.). They had a completely different take on race. An eleven-year-old being raised in whitey-white town told Hagerman that racism "was a problem when all those slaves were around and that like bus thing . . . like Eleanor Roosevelt, and how she went on the bus. And she was African American and sat on the white part . . . but after the 1920s and all that, things changed." And while this shining example of the American educational complex is delivering his oration, the parents of this poor child stood by smiling proudly.

And it's that smile, those nods, the doing and not the saying, that affects these children's worldviews the most. They're the thumb on the scale, according to Hagerman. "Everyday behaviors of white parents also matter: when to lock the car doors, what conversations to have at the dinner table, what books and magazines to have around the house, how to react to news headlines, who to invite over for summer cookouts, whether and how to answer questions posed by kids about race, who parents are friends with themselves, when to roll one's eyes, what media to consume, how to respond to overtly racist remarks made by Grandpa at a family dinner and where to spend leisure time," she continued in *Time*.

"The conversations parents have with their white children about race and racism matter—it's just that so does everything else parents do. Rather than focusing solely on what they *say* to kids about race, white parents should think more critically and carefully about how what they *do* on an everyday basis may actually reproduce the very racist ideas and forms of racial inequality that they say they seek to challenge," concluded Hagerman.

Parents might not even be aware of what they're doing. That their involuntary racist tics are teaching their children who matters and who doesn't. But our kids are freaking creepers, man. They are always watching, listening, absorbing. Black Mamas know this. We been known it. It's why when Sally chases a white girl who doesn't want to play, I step in and fill the vacuum with all good vibes. Rob asked what I wanted Racist Elsa to know, and the answer I couldn't muster then becomes clear—that she doesn't get to decide my child's day; she is not the sun. I want her to know that just as much as I want Sally to. Even though it's not *my* job to teach this little white girl what's up, if I don't then two decades from now she'll grow into a problem I can't fix with a snarky comeback. A problem Sally might meet in a place where I can't protect her. Hagerman emphasizes that white parents need to be the change, basically, but for Black parents, even if we're actively saying *and* doing all the things that matter, the world can erase all our hard work in an instant. Or at least that's the fear that's always lurking underneath nearly all our parenting choices. Man, that's heavy.

The talk? More like talks, or the talk that never ends. We prep for it. We've spent a lifetime gathering notes. And yet, when it arrives it takes our breath away.

"I wish my face was different," Sally tells me one morning while inspecting herself in the bathroom mirror.

"Huh?" I manage, nearly choking on the pink-flavored Paw Patrol toothpaste she'd begged me to try. Damn. We're here? Already? Baby girl continues examining her contours with that psycho intensity only four-year-olds can pull off—caressing her tawny cheeks with her tiny hands and making long *O*s with her mouth to stretch every inch of her perfect skin.

Still staring at her reflection, my child says, "I want my skin to be another color."

Ring the alarm! Someone alert whatever secret MIB-type agency revokes Black Mama cards because, guys, I have failed! This baby, who I have purposefully placed in a Black-girl-magic echo chamber with Beyoncé surround sound, wants Different. Colored. Skin. What do I do? Who do I call? Where are the instructions?

"Goose, what are you talking about? Your skin is everything! It's brown like Mommy's. Like Yaya's. Like Memaw's," I counter, trying not to sound hysterical. "It's beautiful."

I swear my heartbeat slows in anticipation of the dagger. The water filling up the bathroom sink for Sally's morning "experiments" stops rising. The wind blowing in from the rip in the window screen pauses. *This is it,* I think. This is the moment when my beautiful baby girl tells me she wants to be white, and I die inside. "What other color would you want it to be?"

My daughter slowly turns to face me and delivers her answer with a devilish grin: "Purple."

CHAPTER **10**

What's in a Name?

When motherhood is new and you're battling hormones, the necessity of comrades-in-arms can't be overstated. So much so that the term "mom friend" is instantly understandable. It is shorthand for everything—support, space-filler, sounding board, breastfeeding expert, postpartum cheerleader, competition, judgment, everything. But as necessary as they are, mom friends can also be ephemeral, forgotten when the babies become full-fledged people, when the address changes or when the smoke clears. That's when the strength of whatever bonds you've forged in the inferno of infant care are truly tested. The Mamas were no exception, especially after the world was lit ablaze again and again, like those trick birthday candles no one thinks are funny.

The first test came after George Floyd's murder. Race, a topic that until then had been kept out of most polite conversation, was now front and center for *them*—if only temporarily. Our neighborhood, filled with the kind of "good white folks" you hear older Black folk make mention of, began organizing socially distanced

marches down First Street (the very staging ground white homeowners had used to intimidate their Black neighbors a century
before) in support of the Black Lives Matter movement. But once
they took a beat and realized a mass gathering wasn't exactly Covid-
friendly, supporters settled for sitting out on their renovated front
porches and banging on pots and things, making a racket for racial
injustice to put God only knows on notice. It was something. I
guess. We stayed inside, though, their liberal indignation quietly
thumping through our closed windows.

"This is some white people shit," I hissed at Rob while distract-
ing the girls with *Daniel Tiger's Neighborhood.*

"Ummhmm."

"Like, what do they think this is going to do? Besides keep folk
up and scare a few rats!" I could be righteous and indignant too,
falling back on the inner opening monologues I used to dole out to
neighbors I didn't know when we first arrived in Bloomingdale. It'd
been years, but that sinking feeling, the Secret White Meeting feeling, that creaking trapdoor, wouldn't go away. Even when you knew
they meant well—pats on the back, joining in—it was more than I
could do.

Take this one mama, Colleen, who is the only white person on
the planet I would unironically describe as woke, to interested
aliens. Her daughter went to a regular daycare and Colleen had no
qualms about her being "the only one" in a center filled mostly with
kids who spoke Spanish at home. And by "no qualms" I mean she
didn't bring it up for clout around *us.* It just was. In fact, for a long
time I thought Colleen was actually a white-passing Latina, since
her daughter's name was Carmen and she almost always gravitated
to the handful of moms of color at any given neighborhood event.
She must be one of us, I thought. But then, at a building tour during
the school lottery craze, Colleen rolled her eyes when a member of
the PTA explained through tears that she was so happy her son

attended a school where he got to "interact with such a diverse group of people." Colleen texted me during this passionate speech, "Is this lady serious? I am so secondhand embarrassed for all white people right now." I liked her.

Anyway, during Bloomingdale's BLM awakening Colleen was very on top of things, like all of us type-A intensive mothers, messaging me when there would be another pot-banging or asking if our family wanted to join hers at a march on the National Mall. I responded with what I hoped was polite and noncommittal encouragement until one day (after another invite) I sort of cracked. "Yeah, we aren't leaving this house with all these crazy fucking white people everywhere. And definitely not taking the girls. We just don't feel safe." It was getting to be too much: the sudden awareness, not just from Colleen, who'd always been down, but from all the parents who'd been more than happy to laugh nervously and change the subject just six months before. To her credit, Colleen responded thoughtfully, "I completely understand and really need to check my own assumption about what's safe and manageable for people going through this." I don't give out gold stars, and she wasn't fishing for any, but still. It was rare in a place like ours to not only feel seen but heard. I took her out of my overflowing "nice white parents" file and put her into the skinny but growing "she cool" file.

And speaking of the Super Cool Moms. Already the WhatsApp group had decided to take matters into its own hands and fix the problem of white supremacy with the help of Microsoft. Did you know Excel spreadsheets can solve systemic racism? No? Well, that didn't stop Carly from spending an enormous number of her billable hours crafting the spreadsheet to end all spreadsheets. Guys, it was just a fucking list of children's books with people of color in them. That was it. And yet there were multiple tabs. Information about age appropriateness. Whether said book was fiction or non.

When to read it to your kids. Where to buy from: preferably one of the few remaining small indie bookstores run by a BIPOC who was probably pushed out of a rapidly gentrifying neighborhood not unlike the one we all called home. There was also an additional resources tab pointing to TED Talks. TED Motherfucking Talks, y'all. Links to articles, documentaries, how to get involved with organizations doing the work. I exaggerate but it was epic. Or at least I imagined it to be because I didn't read it. Refused to, actually.

As the only Black mom in the group, I felt it my duty to ignore all messages about "the spreadsheet." This was their burning cross to douse in water, not mine. It felt surreal, of course—having a group of some of your closest mom friends, most of them white, "talk" (i.e., text) around you about the best strategies to raise non-racist kids. Okay, fine, maybe I virtually raised my hand a few times to point out that owning a bunch of board books about slavery and civil rights was exactly the problem. Do you really want your tod-dler to think Black people exist in a constant struggle loop of oppression and overcoming and firsts? How 'bout they live their regular degular lives like everyone else? Just pepper your bookshelf with faces other than your own. How hard is that? Very. These weren't the kind of women to combat a global pandemic, racial injus-tice, and social upheaval with a hashtag. They needed to *do* some-thing. And trust I got it. Remember we were all the daughters. So, the spreadsheet.

I never fully understood the term "virtue signaling," but I felt like this was it. I silently pouted about it. I stomped my foot. Why? Because slaying racism felt like all the other things we'd been doing for years—music class, baby yoga, toddler ballet lessons, etc. It was all lumped in together and that left a lump in my throat. Lynn O'Brien Hallstein, the motherhood expert, agreed.

"Who's not on board with that? Their intentions seem to be right. 'I've got to get the right books and teach them the right things.' It's about how do I find all these resources. But it's an example of mothers going into overdrive. That's such a classic response from a certain type of mother. The first impulse is not to do something on the ground, it's like, 'What book should I get?' I say that as one of those moms," she said. Clearly, so was I. Of course, the goodly mothers of my neighborhood became as obsessed with teaching their kids how to not be racist as they were with teaching them the sign for "milk." Because this is what we did. It was all of a piece. "Wheels on the Bus" and reverse-white-supremacist indoctrination. They approached the task like any type-A, D.C., I-read-The-1619-Project mom would: with stuff and things and planning and PayPal.

Also, what else did I expect them to do? At least they were searching for something, at least they knew what they didn't know. And they knew not to bug me with their questions about how to do better. They were going to figure it out on their own. In fact, Leah sent me a private message, letting me know that she was thinking of my family as the country's approach to race seemed malleable and protests were now morning news. Around that same time, a Black mom friend joked that I'd have to leave "the Karen Moms Group Chat." But they weren't that—Karens, I mean. I never saw them that way. They were those fucking girls but not *those* fucking girls. *The New York Times* defined "Karen" as "an epithet for a type of interfering, hectoring white woman, the self-appointed hall monitor, unloosed on the world, so assured of her status in society that she doesn't hesitate to summon the authorities—demanding to speak to the manager or calling the police—for the most trivial and often wholly imaginary transgressions." Karens these women were not. In fact, that Excel spreadsheet, as much as it gave me an emotional paper cut, was proof that they were at least thinking past their own noses.

Remember that 2007 study of kindergartners and their families in the *Journal of Marriage and Family* that Dani McClain quoted in her *Atlantic* article? Three out of four white parents said they avoided the topic of race entirely, considering the mere mention of racial difference as itself racist. That's how you get these dummies who say they "don't see color." Yes the hell you do, you're just scared that seeing means something worse. But we can't leave our (their) kids to their own devices. Otherwise, you get Racist Elsa and her cast of tiki-torch-wielding Disney friends.

According to a 2020 study co-authored by Jessica Sullivan and Leigh Wilton, both assistant professors of psychology at Skidmore College, many white parents think the golden age to broach the topic of race and racism is five. But kids are ready long before that.

"Even if it's a difficult topic, it's important to talk with children about race, because it can be difficult to undo racial bias once it takes root," explained Wilton in an article published by the American Psychological Association. "Toddlers can't do calculus, but that doesn't mean we don't teach them to count. You can have a conversation with a toddler about race that is meaningful to them on their level." Basically, you have to start somewhere.

Case in point: the spreadsheet. I wanted to hate on it—a collection of kids' books about how not to be terrible—but how could I? How could anyone? Was this not what everyone was *supposed* to be doing now? Recognizing your privilege and not passing it on to the next generation? Wasn't this a good thing these women were doing? Trying to make the world a better place and all? Didn't Band Dad need this list? And whoever Racist Elsa was calling mama? Probably. Okay, fine, yes definitely. But tell that to my rolling eyes. Because in the back of my mind all I could think was, "Of course, noooow you're concerned. But what's gonna happen when the latest parenting craze goes the way of the Tiger Mom. Who would be left with the FFPPU Whole Foods paper bag full of nonracist Montessori toys?" Remember what Denene Millner, the author and publisher dedicated to telling joyful stories about Black children, said? When push comes to shove, *their* impetus to be better is fragile. "It's there for the moment, but the second it feels uncomfortable? They're done." So maybe that's why I resisted diving into that spreadsheet at first; I didn't want to get hurt when water ran dry or, worse, be the recipient of my own "I told you so" when it happened. This was just another trapdoor disguised as a bridge. And did you see *Squid Games* (the *s* added for Blackness)?

Mixed in with that fear was the fact that ain't nobody asked me for my Black-ass opinion. The hell? I scrolled and scrolled but no one did the thing where everyone turns to the one Black girl in the room and tests, "Soooo what do *you* think?" That was a good thing, right? Because it wasn't my job to teach these women about the invisible diaper bag! But what other Black mothers did they know?! Had I not been cast in this play as Black Mom Friend No. 1? And it was that thought, that thought right there, that made me realize how much of my own shit—privilege, racial guilt, urban fatigue, financial insecurity, acute impostor syndrome, and social pressure— I had to deal with. None of these women had ever put me into the Black Friend box; I'd crawled in myself. I felt comfortable there— I knew the rules, the red flags—but still complained about how tight the space was.

So, yeah, I opened that stupid fucking spreadsheet. It had forty-one book recommendations. Y'all, I owned exactly two. Two! What did that say about me? How Black was I really? I hadn't marched, under the pretext that my big-ass Black husband would be a target. I hadn't donated, because student loans. I hadn't posted on Facebook, because journalist. What *had* I done? Sure, these women were white (and Korean, and Chinese, and South Asian) AF, but was I as Black as I claimed to be? I'd been intensive mothering and cultivating and helicoptering with the best of them for years. I'd damn near come to blows with a kindergartner at the playground

for ignoring my obviously perfect Black daughter. I'd acted as a
magnet for Black moms who'd finally, blessedly made their way
back to our hood and made sure to pass along every bit of information I got from showing up to the Secret White Meetings. I was
parenting like a motherfucker. But *aht aht aht,* I could hardly pat
myself on the back yet. Two? Two.

There was one particular book on the list that raised a few questions. Leah was reading it to one of her three-year-old daughters. It
featured a multicultural cast of characters on the cover and was
supposed to be teaching its toddler audience about unconscious
bias.

"It confused Deena so much. She asked me to explain it to her,
like, thirty-five times."

On one page the book explained that racism can sometimes be
by "mistake," like asking the same dark-skinned friend to always
play the robber during cops and robbers. I mean, *we* got it, but
Leah's preschooler didn't, because she had no clue that Black meant
bad—yet. It was a chicken-and-egg situation, and Leah was
stumped. Do you introduce the problem of racism to a three-year-
old or do you wait until she learns about it from some QAnon kid
on the monkey bars? White parents so often go for the easy road
because they can. Close the book and choose another. The research
says that's a no-no.

"I felt so stuck trying to explain it," admitted Leah, but at least
she was muscling through. It reminded me of the line that my
friend Shilpi used to wrap up the neighborhood and its many first-
world foibles—"Everyone is trying."

The group had always been a kind of bubble, but then it popped.
Now we talked about racism as much as it came up, which was
often, starting with that fiery summer when a man was killed, guns
went off, and folks marched, and into the next year when a Black
woman became the first female vice president of the United States

and white folks got so mad they stormed the capitol. It was a lot, and we couldn't hide from it. Motherhood in our gentrified neighborhood was no longer a Polly Pocket world of postracialism. (And when I say that, I mean for white people. Black parents ain't never been postracial.) If anything, motherhood was now a microscope. Like how all of a sudden the kids mutually agreed that sleep was for suckers and everyone's kid was waking up at an ungodly hour in the morning. It was the second week of January 2021. As usual we gave each other advice on the brutal transition from one nap to none and wake times and blah, blah, blah. Then Nancy said what we all should have: "I wonder if they're responding to the anxiety we've all been feeling since the sixth?" *Ding ding ding.*

This opened up a long conversation about the doomsday news following "the events of January sixth." Did we let our kids watch? Was that the responsible thing to do for a parent trying to raise antiracist kids? Or was it abuse? Why on earth would a preschooler need to see white people raging against democracy on CNN? But shouldn't we be talking about it?

"When Trump got into office, my goal was to make it four years with the kids never knowing who the president was. Two. More. Weeks," wrote Carly, who knew other mom friends who were adamant about mixing cable news with cartoons.

"I think a lot of this 'Talk to your kids' crap is white guilt, honestly," I wrote, because I felt comfortable enough among these very specific white women to just say the quiet part out loud.

"Yes *this,*" wrote Meghan. "A sorority sister of mine who posts a lot of performative parenting BS sent me a picture of her two-year-old staring at MSNBC, and I'm like, why?"

Leah agreed but offered up another perspective worth thinking about: "A lot of people, me included, are also responding to the fact that white kids have the privilege of growing up without having to deal with racism at all. So we're trying to educate them . . . but the whole 'Sit them in front of the news thing'? Oy." Everybody's trying.

Our WhatsApp group became a place where we could speak freely and without a lot of filter. Not explaining ourselves to one another but unburdening ourselves. Seeing sides we didn't see before. We talked about whether folks should point out someone's skin color or race to their kids in books and on TV. Or was that racist? (No, by the way.) Which then led to a conversation about colorism, an issue that touched Angie and Priya's lives in a way I had never considered. Light skin versus dark skin was a *School Daze* Bollywood dance number they were deeply familiar with. White privilege had seeped into all of our lives. Talking it out was no longer taboo. But if I'm being honest, sometimes I missed the blissful ignorance. I wanted to stick an "out to lunch" sign on the door of all these open-door conversations, which is what happened when deep into the pandemic Colleen sent me and my friend Monica this email:

"Can we talk about these friggin' pods? Are either of you thinking about joining or starting one? If so, can we do one together? I'm sure there's an afterschool teacher or former nanny in need of work right now, you know. Just a thought! Would love to hash it out more if you're interested."

Listen, I liked her. Like for real. Even after I found out she wasn't a light-skinned Cuban woman. She was the kind of white person who instead of apologizing for their privilege decided to disrupt it as best she could. I would describe it as refreshing if I didn't want to give kudos for, you know, being a decent human. It was clear Colleen really wanted to be friends. Not just mom friends but for-real friends. But because she seemed so thoughtful about race, in a neighborhood like ours, I was suspicious. In the back of my mind there was this itching. Did she want to be friends because she truly liked me or because she wanted her daughter to have a Black childhood bestie to claim when she was arguing down some racist eigh-teen years from now or on the presidential-debate stage in thirty? And even if that was the case, would that be so bad?

Another concept laid out in Margaret Hagerman's *White Kids: Growing Up with Privilege in a Racially Divided America* is a theory she called the "conundrum of privilege." It asserts that parents who have a lot of resources because of their economic status and their whiteness obviously want to choose "the best" option available to them. In a racist society those options are usually lily white (schools, social circles, health care, etc.). That's just good parenting, right? Giving your kid "the best" of everything. And if that category just so happens to paint their world in black and white, well, too bad. Them's the breaks. The conundrum lies with those parents who *also* believe in multiculturalism, who want their children to dismantle the system and live in an egalitarian society sans systemic racial oppression. To practice what you preach in that regard might mean choosing the second best or third best for your kid. Colleen was sending her daughter to the local school, which was majority Black, and she was making a conscious effort to befriend Black folks in her world, which, sociologists have repeatedly emphasized, greatly impacts how white children see the world. She was doing the right thing, and I was squinty-eyed about it because no one ever does.

So anyway, pods. Colleen emailed me and Monica, who you'll remember is also Black, about joining hers. Thing is, Mon and I had started a separate group chat weeks before with a dozen or so Black moms, the same women we hosted regular Black Kid Take-overs with at Crispus Attucks. We convened online for the express purpose of possibly starting one of these things for our own kids. Because if we had to create a school out of whole cloth, why not make it as Black on Black on Black as we could?

"Do you wanna tell her? Or should I?" I texted Monica after see-ing Collen's email.

Her reply: ¯_(ツ)_/¯

The mere idea of our all-Black "Should we do this ridic pod thing like these white folks?" online exploratory committee felt revolutionary. Then Colleen's email made me feel bad about it. Was I excluding her? Was this the "reverse racism" all those tiki-torch buffoons be carrying on about? Did I give a damn if it was? It wasn't. But for a while, my strategy had been to scroll past that email until Colleen hopefully moved down her list of POC moms to befriend. Okay, that's really unfair. Isn't that what we want white women to be doing? Reaching out to mothers who don't look like them? And after stewing about the spreadsheet, wasn't I the one avoiding tough conversations now?

That's when I realized how much my mom-friend cup ranneth over. "You and your mommy groups," one of my old pals chided with what sounded like a wee bit of jealousy. I had the Mamas, the Super Cool Moms, and my Black mom friends. Never was the difference clearer than in the middle of the pandemic. We now had the power (and privilege) to curate our kids' socially distant lives from scratch, and if that was the case, why not bubble-wrap them up in safety, i.e., away from white kids? The Black Kids Pod listserv, which was admittedly not very big, started strong but would fizzle out once we realized (yet again) that being Black and a mother didn't necessarily mean we wanted the same exact things for our kids. Dawn Marie Dow had identified three different types of Black middle-class mothers in her book *Mothering While Black,* and trust we had a rep for each category and more yet to be discovered. There were moms who wanted as much outdoor time as possible. Others were "big into" dual language and pondered whether we could hire someone who spoke French. I, on the other hand, just wanted my kid out of the house long enough for me to be able to answer more than one Slack message an hour and maybe take a meeting without resorting to throwing flip-flops off camera. Things fell apart once we realized how complex the logistics were (and who had the time), but the core group, the one I'd been gathering since Tess mysteriously evaporated and suddenly Lynne (and Monica, Denise, Amber, and Chi) showed up to take her place, remained tight, and to this day we still plot our children's success together.

Eventually Colleen found some folks to pod with via the Mamas, because all roads always led back to the Mamas—which, by the way, we weren't even calling "the Mamas" anymore, it was now "the Bdale Parents" group. Oh, the drama involved! Like the dumbest non-Covid-related or non-life-threatening—and therefore useless— internet drama of all time. And the only women I could safely and reliably bitch to about how stupid the change was were Meghan, Carly, Leah, Mira, and the crew, the Super Cool Moms of Whatsapp, who were as invested in this silly shit as I was. Here's how it hit the fan the first time.

Really, it was bound to happen at some point. In the five years since its inception as a small collection of neighborhood moms stumbling through the first few months of sleep deprivation together, the Mamas Facebook group had grown from a few dozen members to nearly seven hundred. It was only a matter of time before the FFPPU and ISO posts would give way to heavier fodder like LGBTQIA allyship and whether all these women were *allowing* men to fully participate in the mental load of parenting, since by definition mom groups are just for, well, moms. Yes, that was the great debate. It was all over the name.

"Good morning, Mamas! This group has been such a big help to me since becoming a mom and moving to the neighborhood. It's awesome! But shouldn't we be a bit more inclusive? Does anyone have a problem with changing the name from Mamas to Parents? Just a thought!" posted a woman who I'm sure had no idea of the shit storm she was about to whip up.

Here we go.

It was a slow Pandemic Monday when this innocent poster decided to blow up our quiet corner of the internet. She hit send at 9 A.M. By 9:15 there were something like a hundred comments from lesbian mothers who said the name was exclusionary, a dad who said he never felt welcome in the group (it's a moms group!), and more than a few mothers who said they wouldn't feel comfortable sharing intimate details about their pelvic floors if somebody else's husband was reading about it. One said she was concerned about "breastfeeding posts." Another replied with a "calm reminder" that trans men and nonbinary parents do not identify with breastfeeding since they don't have breasts but they do in fact chestfeed their hungry babies. Yep, that's how this was going.

"I am out. The comments against changing the name to be more inclusive of queer and trans families are shocking to me. And who wouldn't want dads to play a more active role? I'm appalled, and I'll be leaving," wrote one mom, who did just that.

To me, the real argument for changing the name, behind the unassailable veil of "inclusion" and virtue signaling, was about forcing the invisible labor of the nanny search, clothes donations, baby-class schedules, etc. on the men who didn't want it no matter what the group called itself. As if changing a name would somehow undo centuries of patriarchy. "Oh, the group's name is changed now, honey, so please schedule the doctor's appointment, cook a rainbow-colored Instagram-worthy dinner for the kids, research the most enriching summer camp, and have it all on the table by five." That, of course, did not happen.

We, the moms of the internet, argued for hours about whether women deserved their own safe space or whether women were selfishly guarding all the gold.

"I highly doubt renaming a Facebook group my husband doesn't know anything about will incentivize the man to remember what size diapers our kids wear or whether or not my old nursing bras are in the donation pile," wrote another mom.

I was surprised by how angry this entire virtual debate made me. Men! In *our* group. Hell to the no! Surprised at just how fiercely— after years of making fun of these women, feeling like an outsider among them, and then finally sorta kinda maybe letting them grow on me—I wanted to protect this air bubble of raw motherhood. Here I could post about the silly mundane aspects of mothering that my own friends never cared about, like Sally eating the sides of her crib and possibly having pica or Robyn not clapping at six months and therefore being a lost cause. I mean, my other friends cared, of course. But how many texts could they respond to? I needed instant gratification for the minutiae of mothering and the Mamas was that. I didn't want to let it go, or more accurately I didn't want it taken away. Because, let's be honest, boys do ruin everything.

The Mamas had become an integral part of my identity as not just a mother, but a woman, a wife, a professional, and a Washingtonian—all of it. We'd forged a connection through story-telling. The ones we told each other. The ones we told ourselves. The truth of who we were was somewhere in between. It was obvious after years of free mom-group therapy that I needed them—but *definitely* not their husbands.

"This is just a way for men to control female spaces," chimed in Rob when I told him about the Great Name Change Debate of 2020. I almost had a seizure. *My* husband, king of "Is dinner ready?," was advocating for a dadsplaining-free zone. Sure, it meant he would never post about lottery results or ask for advice on potty training, but would he ever?

I'd spent three years of my life giving pieces of myself—great and small—to this group, and I'd be damned if some dude came and pissed all over it. And thankfully the Super Cool Moms agreed with me. More proof that our tight-knit group was cut from the same cloth.

"This is so dumb," wrote Mira as we all watched the virtual debate unfold over proverbial popcorn. "I'm going to leave a comment, you guys back me up." We all left comments, pointing to the fact that making a space "for women" didn't make it "against men." No one was advocating for dads to be summarily kicked out of the group. There were plenty of fathers (okay, two) who posted on the regular. But this wasn't *about* them. It was about us.

When someone effectively accused Carly of being "unneighborly" things really went off the rails. It was like calling her a raging racist. I mean, no, but in this context the emotional stakes were climbing fast.

The debate scrolled on and inevitably included some mansplaining from one of the involved dads. (That did not go over well.) The group's administrator, bowing to pressure or maybe just overwhelmed by how much time a bunch of random women had on their hands, had changed the name to Bdale Parents by the end of the day—which, let's be honest, if you want to be inclusive: Not all caregivers are "parents," but tomayto, tomahto, I guess. The next morning the mansplainer posted "a question for dads" about strollers for tall people. No one responded.

"I'm getting a lot of satisfaction out of that," wrote Leah in WhatsApp.

The group passed that trial by fire, though just barely. It still stands, unlike other Facebook groups for "moms" (in quotes since it's allegedly now for everyone despite the fact that, one year after the Great Name Change, 99.9 percent of the posts are for and by women mothering children). There are several online forums in name-brand cities that have imploded under the weight of the really big questions. Like, what is this group for, who does it center on, and who is excluded?

The famed Longest Shortest Time Mamas Facebook group was founded in 2014, not long before the Mamas, and two years later was shut down. Praised as a supportive corner for mom struggles, it had ballooned to nearly twenty thousand members in no time, and when the frank discussions devolved and turned the group from safe space to battlefield, its founder, podcaster Hillary Frank, shut it down. The *New York Post* wrote a story about the implosion of the UES Mommas, an online group of forty thousand members, that was roiled when "the usual conversations about diaper rash turned to difficult discussions about race." *The New York Times* covered the story too. Was this a beat now? Mom groups gone wild. Thankfully none of that happened to the Parents, née Mamas. That is, until one of the Super Cool Moms asked that a moderator be added, and another Great Big Argument on the internet ensued.

Again, this was dumb, okay? We realize that. Drama online has no real bearing on your real life, or does it? If the lessons from any of the other groups being shuttered were to be taken to heart, the Bdale Parents needed policing. Or at the very least a stern hall monitor, who made sure folks didn't say some slick shit to one another. So one morning without warning Nancy, whose no-nonsense bluntness I was in awe of, sprung another pop quiz on the group. She asked that the administrator, the same woman who'd unceremoniously changed our name and who, as it so happens, had moved out of the state years before, add more administrators to help keep the peace in uncertain times. Nancy's Facebook poll—yes, she had a poll ready—was a surprise for sure, but not unwarranted.

Of the hundreds of people in the group, sixty-seven of us voted for more administrators, twenty-seven voted to make the group private but "searchable," and three voted to leave things alone. It did not go over well. The administrator felt bullied and attacked. "I don't have the time for this, guys. Mean-girl shenanigans like this should be reserved for DC Urban Moms not Bdale Parents." The administrator went on to say that those who didn't like how the group was run could start their own group. What's funny is that that exact phrase rears its ugly head in every other slash-and-burn Facebook mom group debate. "Start your own group!" Every single one. I won't say that it sounds a lot like "Go back to your own country!," especially when it is so often lobbed at people of color who dare to question the status quo of a space that wasn't necessarily made for them but is a space they exist in anyhow. Nancy, remember, is Korean American. I won't say it sounds like what the white mob politely told Bloomingdale's first Black homeowners back in 1923. I won't say how offensive it is. How ultimately racist it can sound. But I'll type that shit, though.

And really, why didn't we just "start our own group"? We already had the Super Cool Moms. I had Black Mom Takeover. We had people. But this group, this space, was the mother ship and we wanted it to feel like home too. Maybe that was the problem. Like recent college graduates we'd outgrown our childhood bedroom, and the Mamas, like all our mamas, were sick of us complaining about the lumpy twin bed. Go live on your own!

What's more—and also how I justified how much emotional energy I was spending on this stupidness—the issue of searchability was clearly exclusionary, and we'd just had this conversation six months before when the name was changed. Dads and LGBTQIA caregivers were up in arms about the group not being inclusive because of the name, but where were they when folks brought up the fact that only friends of current members could find the group on Facebook, which meant that basically all the members of the "go-to parenting resource" of the neighborhood were largely from the same socioeconomic group and, well, white. Did Major's dad know about Bdale Parents? The mom of the kid who Lynne kicked out of the playground? The folks who could actually use all the expensive "slightly used" kids' gear we traded back and forth for nothing, the spreadsheets packed with free activities around town for families, the deep dissection of school choice and the best charters. Who was this group for? Who was a Mama, er Parent, or whatever?

"Like, if we're talking about this place already being divided, then making the group only based on word of mouth seems to make that worse, right?" asked Leah in WhatsApp.

"God, this whole thing is the worst," I wrote back.

"It feels so gross that we're all patting ourselves on the back about donating to mutual aid in the group, but these same people don't want it open to everyone who lives here," typed Meghan.

Was this it? The death rattle? Not the racial reckoning, not the name change, but this? Someone asking to be seen and the powers that be saying, "Yeah, no." Was this the end of the Mamas for me and my friends? The final test that, should the group pass or fail, would determine where we truly felt like members of the motherhood tribe? That was the thing. Once the pandemic forced us closer, the lemon squeeze revealed some uncomfortable truths. Like the fact that some of these moms were a wee bit less liberal than their pussy hats would have you believe.

After a long debate, the group's administrator elevated three new members to admin status. Every single one was a white woman. Insert Nancy Pelosi clap here.

We bitched about it in WhatsApp. "I am shaking right now," wrote Tina, who'd argued with a well-meaning white woman who suggested she Facebook-friend strangers on the street in order to get them into the group. "Thanks for telling me how to behave in your neighborhood, not ours, yours," clapped back Tina. Also, this was

at the height of #StopAsianHate. "Ugh, this fucking group," wrote
Nancy, which reminded me of all my own angst about "those fucking girls." Once again, we complained to one another and were
comforted by the fact that at least *we* got it. At least we knew where
the cracks were. We knew that everyone in the Mamas wasn't our
kinda mama. The Super Cool Moms, though, was a brain trust. We
knew each other. This was the gang gang! Right? Wrong. There was
a traitor in our midst.

Okay, *traitor* is loud. This was not the Revolutionary War. I
mean kinda, but not. Remember Tiffany, the infectious disease
doctor I'd spent countless hours kicking back ciders with, laughing
about how our mothers were basically the same kinda crazy? Turns
out she wasn't the same kind of crazy as the rest of us. She'd remained
oddly quiet when the debate over the administrators unfolded, plus
she had been all for the name change. Come to find out Tiffany was
in fact very close friends with the group's original founder. The plot
thickens! Yes, we know, this is stupid. Explaining internet outrage
to anyone not directly involved is like explaining the sky to deep-
sea fish. They have zero use for it. But the Mamas was like air to
some of us, and when it got polluted with all the "Go start your
own group" talk, we figured everyone should be left gagging. Not
Tiffany, though. She was fine with it, and all but over our new
favorite pastime of poking holes in the larger group's groupthink.

"I'm sorry some of you are triggered and feel othered and that
people I happen to know offended you," wrote Tiffany after a long
Whatsapp group rant about the name change, the admin issue, and
the entire neighborhood's general problem of liberal well-meaning
gentrification.

"Guys, I'm out," she wrote to us unceremoniously after some
back and forth about the current state of the Mamas, nay Parents.
She didn't have time for this. She wished us the best, and the next

message WhatsApp delivered was a verdict: "Tiffany has left the chat."

That was the last (latest) test of this grand friend experiment. It was the first time after years of tap-dancing on the trapdoor that a bona fide member of the Super Cool Moms, my happy place, truly felt out of step. I was shocked it took so long. The rest of us went radio silent for a while. Letting Tiffany's last text hang in the air. "Be well," she had signed off. In my head it sounded like a wish and an indictment. Were we "those fucking girls" to her? Was she protecting herself, poking her head in the sand? Did it even matter? You choose who you choose. Then two days later it was Mother's Day, and we sent one another a bunch of pictures of the dumb pancakes our husbands made us.

When I ran down the whole absurd soap opera to Rob later, his eyes crossed.

"And this is a bunch of grown women doing this?"

"Well, yes."

"And don't y'all have kids to take care of?"

"Yes, and that is not the point!"

"Well, what is?"

This dude and his questions.

In *Big Friendship* Aminatou Sow and Ann Friedman track how they went from besties in their early twenties to estranged and back again. Their story underscores how hard it is to really hold on to people. First, you have to actually like them; second, you have to find the value in maintaining the friendship; and third, you have to work at it. The Mamas, the Super Cool Moms, the Black Mom Takeover, Mocha Moms, PACE, MOPS, La Leche League, the PTA, and all the huddled groups in between could add up to a big friendship, a medium-sized one, or one that was so threadbare it disintegrated in the wash. It was all in the fit.

Were things falling apart as they tend to do? Maybe. Or maybe we were all just getting that much closer to that always elusive authentic self, shedding what didn't serve us and clinging to what did. Because in addition to the Mamas, I now had several groups—online and in person—to turn to. I was no longer that woman, pregnant and afraid, on the sidewalk, watching all the *other* and allegedly better moms doing a dance that looked too complicated to learn. I had people. I had examples. They all reflected different images of the mother, the woman I wanted to be, and none were more important than the other. I was an intensive mother, a gentrifying mother, a mother who respected the ghosts of her block. I was a Black mother; I was a baby yoga evangelist and owner of every children's book with a brown girl on the cover. I was a PTA slacker, the mom who trusted her daughter's otherwise middling preschool teacher because she was a Black woman, and the mom who needed to dig into that Excel spreadsheet. Chaka Khan was a soothsayer. I'm every woman. We are all the daughters. And for me the only way to piece together what success looked like was by exposing myself to all the stuff. It was as if I'd been parenting myself all along. But whether or not I'm doing it right is above me now.

So this isn't really the story of how I ended up the only Black mom in a group filled with white women. It's the story of how a Black mom both carries and shrugs off the albatross of the expectation and judgment that exist in her own head and out in the world with the help of the mothers surrounding her.

I swear I wasn't getting ready to preach today. But I've told this same long-ass story so many times, repeated it to friends who get it and friends who don't. Folks who never thought twice about "the only one" sitting next to them and folks who've never been anything but. It's the same story I started telling our new neighbor, Cyndi. She and her boyfriend moved next door in the early months of the pandemic and promptly got married and pregnant. They were basically the us of three years before.

Cyndi, who was Black, would shyly seek my advice on random mom things when we saw each other on the block. She was navigating her growing belly, and I was yelling at Sally to please use her "walking feet" and for Robyn to stop kicking Miss Connie's gate.

"Who's your pediatrician?" Cyndi asked one day. "And did you have a doula? A chiropractor? I'm thinking of a nanny share, but I'm not sure." She was a fountain, and I knew a good source for more water.

"Are you on Facebook?" I asked her. "Because you have to join the Mamas."

ACKNOWLEDGMENTS

In a book about motherhood, I would be remiss not to first thank my uterus. Despite being terrified of what you could do since, like, the tenth grade, in the end we did that shit. And to the babies who emerged from the aforementioned, Sally and Robyn, you are the only permanent pieces to a puzzle I am constantly rejiggering. Your father deserves some recognition too, I guess. Robert Dyer is a man you can give your dreams to and who gives them back with extra sauce.

The Ross Yoon Agency has been my literary home since I was a baby author, and after book number three, they ain't getting rid of me anytime soon. My editor at Crown, Madhulika Sikka, spent months in my mom brain and helped me make sense of the gobbledygook therein. She got what all this was about even when I sometimes lost the thread underneath loads of mental (and actual) laundry and whatever the hell else writer-mother-wives are dealing with.

Slow clap for all the Mamas, the women who didn't ask to hop on my emotional motherhood roller coaster but who were more or less down for the ride. Thank you for being so unapologetically yourselves (free advice, problematic Facebook posts, and all), because it made me see something I was missing: None of us know what we're doing, and we all need "people" to fumble through the instructions with.

BIBLIOGRAPHY

"Catholic University Graduations Draws a Large Audience." *The Evening Star,* June 8, 1898.

Cherkasky, M., and S. J. Shoenfeld. National Register of Historic Places Registration Application. Washington, D.C., March 21, 2021.

Cherkasky, Mara. Personal interview. April 27, 2021.

Dill, LeConté. "The Fourth of You Lie." Zócalo Public Square, May 19, 2021.

Dow, Dawn Marie. *Mothering While Black: Boundaries and Burdens of Middle-Class Parenthood.* Berkeley: University of California Press, 2019.

Epstein, R., J. J. Blake, and T. González. "Girlhood Interrupted: The Erasure of Black Girls' Childhood." Center on Poverty and Inequality: Georgetown Law, 2017.

Friedman, Aminatou, and Ann Sow. *Big Friendship: How We Keep Each Other Close.* New York: Simon & Schuster, 2020.

Gonda, Jeffrey D. *Unjust Deeds: The Restrictive Covenant Cases and the Making of the Civil Rights Movement.* Chapel Hill: The University of North Carolina Press, 2015.

Hagerman, Margaret. "Why White Parents Need to Do More Than Talk to Their Kids About Racism." *Time,* September 4, 2018.

————. *White Kids: Growing Up with Privilege in a Racially Divided America*. New York: NYU Press, 2018.

Hays, Sharon. *The Cultural Contradictions of Motherhood*. New Haven: Yale University Press, 1996.

Hill Collins, Patricia. *Black Feminist Thought: Knowledge, Consciousness, and the Politics of Empowerment*. London: Routledge, 2009.

Klein, Melissa. "Upper East Side Moms Facebook Group Implodes After Intense Diversity Fight." *New York Post*, June 6, 2020.

Lareau, Annette. *Unequal Childhoods: Class, Race, and Family Life*, 2nd ed. Berkeley: University of California Press, 2011.

————. Personal interview. May 5, 2021.

Malinowski, Shilpi. Personal interview. April 8, 2021.

McClain, Dani. "What's Lost When Black Children Are Socialized into a White World." *The Atlantic*, November 21, 2019.

Millner, Denene. Personal interview. April 21, 2021.

Mishan, Ligaya. "The March of the Karens." *The New York Times*, August 12, 2021.

Moore, Katrina. Personal interview. May 12, 2021.

Murray wedding cards. *The Washington Times*, September 29, 1909.

Myers Asch, Chris, and George Derek Musgrove. *Chocolate City: A History of Race and Democracy in the Nation's Capital*. Chapel Hill: The University of North Carolina Press, 2017.

O'Brien, Lynn. Personal interview. March 31, 2021.

O'Reilly, Andrea. Personal interview. April 6, 2021.

Parker, K., and E. Patten. "The Sandwich Generation: Rising Financial Burdens for Middle-Aged Americans." Pew Research Center, January 30, 2013.

Philyaw, Deesha. Personal interview. March 24, 2021.

Pinker, Susan. *The Village Effect: How Face-to-Face Contact Can Make Us Healthier, Happier, and Smarter.* New York: Spiegel & Grau, 2014.

"Racial 'Protest' Halted by Police." *The Evening Star,* November 7, 1923.

Shoenfeld, S. J. Personal interview. April 27, 2021

Straight, Susan. "Bloomingdale: The Vibrant Community Now Is One of D.C.'s Most-Coveted Addresses." *The Washington Post,* September 23, 2020.

Sullivan, J., L. Wilton, and E. P. Apfelbaum. "Adults Delay Conversations About Race Because They Underestimate Children's Processing of Race." *Journal of Experimental Psychology,* August 6, 2020.

Szekely, Balazs. "Top 20 Most Gentrified ZIP codes 2000–2016." RentCafé.com, February 26, 2018.

Weir, Kirsten. *Raising Anti-racist Children.* American Psychological Association, June 2, 2021.

Williamson, V., J. Gode, and H. Sun. *"We All Want What's Best for Our Kids": Discussions of D.C. Public School Options in an Online Forum.* The Brookings Institution, March 29, 2021.

ABOUT THE AUTHOR

HELENA ANDREWS-DYER is a senior culture writer at *The Washington Post* and the author of *Bitch Is the New Black* and *Reclaiming Her Time: The Power of Maxine Waters.* Her first book was optioned by Shonda Rhimes. Her work has appeared in *O: The Oprah Magazine, Marie Claire, Glamour,* and *The New York Times,* among other publications. Helena has appeared on ABC's *Nightline,* CBS's *This Morning,* CNN, MSNBC, SiriusXM, NPR, and NY1. She lives in Washington, D.C., with a husband whose laugh can be heard for miles and two equally carefree daughters.

Instagram: @helena_andrews
Twitter: @helena_andrews

ABOUT THE TYPE

This book was set in Garamond, a typeface originally designed by the Parisian type cutter Claude Garamond (c. 1500–61). This version of Garamond was modeled on a 1592 specimen sheet from the Egenolff-Berner foundry, which was produced from types assumed to have been brought to Frankfurt by the punch cutter Jacques Sabon (c. 1520–80).

Claude Garamond's distinguished romans and italics first appeared in *Opera Ciceronis* in 1543–44. The Garamond types are clear, open, and elegant.